Building Serverless Architectures

Unleash the power of AWS Lambdas for
your applications

Cagatay Gurturk

BIRMINGHAM - MUMBAI

Building Serverless Architectures

First published: July 2017

Production reference: 1140717

Published by Packt Publishing Ltd.
Livery Place
35 Livery Street
Birmingham
B3 2PB, UK.

ISBN 978-1-78712-919-1

www.packtpub.com

Credits

Author

Cagatay Gurturk

Reviewer

Martin Lindenburg

Commissioning Editor

Aaron Lazar

Acquisition Editor

Chaitanya Nair

Content Development Editor

Siddhi Chavan

Technical Editor

Dhiraj Chandanshive

Copy Editor

Zainab Bootwala

Project Coordinator

Vaidehi Sawant

Proofreader

Safis Editing

Indexer

Aishwarya Gangawane

Production Coordinator

Nilesh Mohite

About the Author

Cagatay Gurturk is a software engineer, internet enterpreneur, and cloud enthusiast.

After finishing his studies at the Istanbul Technical University, he continued his education to get a master's degree in computer engineering at Bahcesehir University. In 2004, in his freshman year at the college, he co-founded Instela, which quickly became one of the most well-known internet platforms in Turkey, with millions of visitors per month. Being the technical co-founder of Instela, he gained experience of running web platforms at scale and was also introduced to the world of cloud computing.

After long years as an internet enterpreneur in Istanbul and Barcelona, he continued his career in different companies, where he delivered software running on cloud infrastructures, especially on AWS. He authored some open source projects related to AWS as well.

He currently works at eBay as a software development manager, and he is also a certified AWS Solutions Architect.

I would like to express my gratitude to the many people who helped and supported me throughout this book, and to all those who read, wrote, offered comments, and assisted me in the editing, proofreading, and designing of this book.

I would like to thank Martin Lindenburg for reviewing every line of this book and bringing his German perfectionism.

I would like to thank Stefano Langenbacher for encouraging me to work on AWS and his belief in serverless computing.

I would like to thank Kaja for all the support she provided me patiently.

And, finally, I would like to thank everyone who motivated me for this work.

About the Reviewer

Martin Lindenburg is a software engineer born in 1982. He grew up in a rural region, about 100 km north of Berlin. He developed his interest in computers and technology at a young age with his brother's Commodore64. Later, he invested all his pocket money to afford his first own 386 computer, where he developed his first programs in Basic and Turbo Pascal to visualize and solve his math homework. This interest evolved, and, a few years later, he finally ended up studying computer engineering in Berlin.

He is now working for more than ten years as a software engineer, and he has worked for companies in the telecommunication group, Deutsche Telekom AG, the financial portal, Wallstreet-Online AG, and the advertisement and affiliate network, ADCELL. He collected experiences from the creation of standalone applications over scalable dynamic webpages with hundreds of users logging in up to millions of daily page views and tracking events.

Currently, he works as a senior software engineer at Home24 and is essentially involved in the integration of serverless architectures and microservices with AWS.

At the same time, he is actively contributing to the open source framework serverless.com and creating open source serverless-plugins.

Thanks to Cagatay Gurturk for letting me review his book and a special thanks to my wife, Maria, and my children, Samuel and Simon, for their patience in the evenings when I had to review new chapters.

www.PacktPub.com

For support files and downloads related to your book, please visit www.PacktPub.com.

Did you know that Packt offers eBook versions of every book published, with PDF and ePub files available? You can upgrade to the eBook version at www.PacktPub.com and as a print book customer, you are entitled to a discount on the eBook copy. Get in touch with us at service@packtpub.com for more details.

At www.PacktPub.com, you can also read a collection of free technical articles, sign up for a range of free newsletters and receive exclusive discounts and offers on Packt books and eBooks.

https://www.packtpub.com/mapt

Get the most in-demand software skills with Mapt. Mapt gives you full access to all Packt books and video courses, as well as industry-leading tools to help you plan your personal development and advance your career.

Why subscribe?

- Fully searchable across every book published by Packt
- Copy and paste, print, and bookmark content
- On demand and accessible via a web browser

Customer Feedback

Thanks for purchasing this Packt book. At Packt, quality is at the heart of our editorial process. To help us improve, please leave us an honest review on this book's Amazon page at https://www.amazon.com/dp/1787129195.

If you'd like to join our team of regular reviewers, you can e-mail us at customerreviews@packtpub.com. We award our regular reviewers with free eBooks and videos in exchange for their valuable feedback. Help us be relentless in improving our products!

Table of Contents

Preface

Over the past few years, all kind of companies, ranging from start-ups to giant enterprises, have started their move to public cloud providers in order to save their costs and reduce the operational effort needed to keep their shops open. While this movement was applied with just a lift and shift strategy, keeping their software architecture the same and only changing where they are hosting it, some companies opted for a mindset change, modifying their software to take advantage of native cloud services other than virtual machines, changing their team structures, and adopting DevOps practices. This opened the door to many changes in the software industry, and it is definitely possible to say that the world after the introduction of cloud computing is not the same as before.

Starting with AWS Lambda's launch in 2014, a new approach to software development came on the scene. Lambda designed to run code pieces responding to external or internal cloud events, without needing to set up any infrastructure upfront, and it brought a real, managed, and pay-per-go infrastructure model. In a short time, the "serverless computing" term was coined, and the same model was adopted by Microsoft, Google, and even IBM in an open source fashion. With the Lambda functions, it is now even possible to craft a complex software system consisting of many independent micro-functions that will run only when they are needed, without needing to maintain individual servers. The Lambda functions can now support a large number of native cloud services, which removes the need of building custom solutions for common needs, and it not only reduces the infrastructure's running and maintenance costs, but also software development costs.

The focus of this book is to design serverless architectures, and weigh the advantages and disadvantages of this approach, along with a few decision factors to consider. You will learn how to design a serverless application, get to know the key points of services that serverless applications are based on, and known issues and solutions. In this book, you will not only learn the AWS Lambda functions, but you will also see how to use the Lambda functions to glue other AWS services together. You will learn how easy it is to build a scalable software system is, taking a CRUD application as an example.

The book addresses key challenges, such as how to slice out the core functionality of the software to be distributed in different cloud services and cloud functions. It covers the basic and advanced usage of these services, testing and securing the serverless software, automating deployment, and more.

Throughout this book, we will only use the Java programming language, and we will build a homegrown deployment system to easily deploy our software.

This book does not intend to cover all the details of the AWS ecosystem, but I believe it will perfectly show you the path through the serverless computing world.

What this book covers

Chapter 1, *Getting Started With Serverless*, introduces you to serverless computing and Lambda functions, sets up the AWS account and environment, and builds the base libraries.

Chapter 2,*Infrastructure as a Code*, teaches you about CloudFormation to define the infrastructure as a code and has the first Lambda function up and running.

Chapter 3, *Hello Internet*, exposes the Lambda function to the internet via the AWS API Gateway.

Chapter 4, *Applying Enterprise Patterns*, implements and configures the dependency injection pattern for the Lambda function.

Chapter 5, *Persisting Data*, uses DynamoDB to persist application data in a highly scalable way.

Chapter 6, *Building Supporting Services*, leverages the AWS services to enable the Lambda functions to pass messages to each other.

Chapter 7, *Searching Data*, uses CloudSearch to build a fully managed search infrastructure, integrating Lambda functions to update the search index.

Chapter 8, *Monitoring, Logging, and Security*, sets up automated health checks, alarms, and triggers responding to failures, and operating Lambda in secured network environments.

Appendix, *Lambada Framework,* migrates your JAX-RS application to AWS Lambda and API Gateway with minimal effort.

What you need for this book

To run all the code in this book, you only need to have the Java Development Kit installed on your machine. You will have to create an AWS account to apply the steps. AWS offers a free tier for new customers that will cover most of the costs of running examples in the book. On the other hand, some services such as CloudSearch and VPC NAT Gateways are not covered by a free tier. Make sure that you visit the pricing documentation of each service used in the book to avoid unnecessary costs.

Who this book is for

This book is for developers and software architects who are interested in designing their software in serverless environments. Since the programming language used in this book is Java, it is preferred that readers are familiar with the basics of Java and the general conventions used in the Java world.

Conventions

In this book, you will find a number of text styles that distinguish between different kinds of information. Here are some examples of these styles and an explanation of their meaning.

Code words in text, database table names, folder names, filenames, file extensions, pathnames, dummy URLs, user input, and Twitter handles are shown as follows: "We can start by adding the next snippet to the `build.gradle` file."

A block of code is set as follows:

```
cloudFormation {
    capabilityIam true
    templateFile project.file('cloudformation.template')
    templateBucket deploymentBucketName
    templateKeyPrefix "cfn-templates"
    stackName "serverlessbook"
}
```

Any command-line input or output is written as follows:

```
$ touch cloudformation.template
```

New terms and **important words** are shown in bold. Words that you see on the screen, for example, in menus or dialog boxes, appear in the text like this: "In order to download new modules, we will go to **Files | Settings | Project Name | Project Interpreter**."

Warnings or important notes appear like this.

Tips and tricks appear like this.

Reader feedback

Feedback from our readers is always welcome. Let us know what you think about this book-what you liked or disliked. Reader feedback is important for us as it helps us develop titles that you will really get the most out of. To send us general feedback, simply e-mail feedback@packtpub.com, and mention the book's title in the subject of your message. If there is a topic that you have expertise in and you are interested in either writing or contributing to a book, see our author guide at www.packtpub.com/authors.

Customer support

Now that you are the proud owner of a Packt book, we have a number of things to help you to get the most from your purchase.

Downloading the example code

You can download the example code files for this book from your account at http://www.packtpub.com. If you purchased this book elsewhere, you can visit http://www.packtpub.com/support and register to have the files e-mailed directly to you. You can download the code files by following these steps:

1. Log in or register to our website using your e-mail address and password.
2. Hover the mouse pointer on the **SUPPORT** tab at the top.
3. Click on **Code Downloads & Errata**.
4. Enter the name of the book in the **Search** box.
5. Select the book for which you're looking to download the code files.
6. Choose from the drop-down menu where you purchased this book from.
7. Click on **Code Download**.

Once the file is downloaded, please make sure that you unzip or extract the folder using the latest version of:

- WinRAR / 7-Zip for Windows
- Zipeg / iZip / UnRarX for Mac
- 7-Zip / PeaZip for Linux

The code bundle for the book is also hosted on GitHub at `https://github.com/PacktPubl ishing/Building-Serverless-Architectures`. We also have other code bundles from our rich catalog of books and videos available at `https://github.com/PacktPublishing/`. Check them out!

Errata

Although we have taken every care to ensure the accuracy of our content, mistakes do happen. If you find a mistake in one of our books-maybe a mistake in the text or the code-we would be grateful if you could report this to us. By doing so, you can save other readers from frustration and help us improve subsequent versions of this book. If you find any errata, please report them by visiting `http://www.packtpub.com/submit-errata`, selecting your book, clicking on the **Errata Submission Form** link, and entering the details of your errata. Once your errata are verified, your submission will be accepted and the errata will be uploaded to our website or added to any list of existing errata under the Errata section of that title. To view the previously submitted errata, go to `https://www.packtpub.com/book s/content/support`and enter the name of the book in the search field. The required information will appear under the **Errata** section.

Piracy

Piracy of copyrighted material on the Internet is an ongoing problem across all media. At Packt, we take the protection of our copyright and licenses very seriously. If you come across any illegal copies of our works in any form on the Internet, please provide us with the location address or website name immediately so that we can pursue a remedy. Please contact us at `copyright@packtpub.com` with a link to the suspected pirated material. We appreciate your help in protecting our authors and our ability to bring you valuable content.

Questions

If you have a problem with any aspect of this book, you can contact us at `questions@packtpub.com`, and we will do our best to address the problem.

1
Getting Started with Serverless

If you are reading this book, you have probably already heard the term **serverless** on more than one occasion. You might have read more than one definition of the term, like every buzzword. I define serverless computing as a new and efficient software development approach that abstracts infrastructure from the functionality itself, letting the developers focus on their business instead of the infrastructure constraints.

I remember myself and my team struggling with these infrastructure constraints in one of the web shops in the late 2000s. After being born as a pet project in college years, Instela had suddenly grown from having hundreds of visits per day to thousands, and we were hosting it on a shared hosting provider. Our website was eating all the CPU available in those poor Xeon servers and our hosting provider unilaterally decided to shut it down to keep neighboring websites up on the same server with us. The local plumber and the coffee shop were online and we were homeless in the cyber world. We did not have any remedy other than running to buy a cheap desktop computer, make it our first server, and bring Instela up again. Our visitor count was increasing day by day, our ATX server was resetting itself a couple of times per day because of overheating, and we ended up buying our first DELL PowerEdge box, which was like a space station for us back in 2005. Everything was cool in the beginning, but as more visitors started to come, our site started to respond slower and slower. Sometimes it was rather fast, and sometimes it was as slow as molasses. Sometimes, there was viral content that attracts thousands of people, and sometimes we had 100 people online. For our data center, it was exactly the same. They were charging us a fixed price and enjoying it. When we needed a new server, we had to spend at least one week, ask whether the local dealer had it in their stock, wait for the delivery, and install the network and the operating system. And what if one of the machines had a hardware issue? We had to wait for the technician and deal with the traffic with one less machine. It was a real pain and there was no other way to run a web platform.

Virtual servers have already existed since the early 2000s, but one can say that real cloud computing started in 2006 with the launch of AWS EC2. It is worth noting that when this service was launched, it was offering very limited options, and for many companies, it was not a production-ready solution.

Nowadays, this horror story is just a legacy to remember for many companies. Public clouds are providing us with a dedicated compute power from their large machine pools. Cloud computing introduced many new concepts and drastically changed how we build and deploy software. We do not have to worry about maintaining an on-premise SAN we mount via NFS. There are S3, Azure Blog Storage, or Google Cloud Storage, which give us the space we really need. We do not monitor the free space or repair it when it is broken. Within the SLA levels, (99.999999999% for AWS S3 [1]) you always know that your storage engine is just there, working. You need a queue service such as RabbitMQ but have AWS Simple Queue Service or Windows Azure Queue Service? You need to implement a search functionality and are planning to deploy an Elasticsearch cluster? You have a managed one: CloudSearch. AWS is offering a managed service even if you are developing a platform that needs to transcode video. You upload your jobs and get the results.

So far, we have spoken about the supporting services that any size of application might need. Leveraging the managed service offerings from public cloud providers, we see that we have become able to shut down some of the servers we previously needed in an on-premise infrastructure. We might say that this is the first part of the serverless architecture. Some authors are calling this type of service **Backend as a Service**, or **BaaS**. However, so far, our software is still running on virtual machines, called instances on AWS and Google Cloud Platform or VMs on Windows Azure. We have to prepare virtual machine images with our application code, spin up instances using them, and configure the auto-scaling rules for cost optimization and scalability. More importantly, we have to pay for these servers on a timely basis, even if you really do not use the reserved compute capacity.

As an alternative to this paradigm, cloud providers came up with the **Functions as a Service (FaaS)** idea. With FaaS, the vast amount of the business logic is still written by the application developer, but they are deployed to fully managed, ephemeral containers that are live only during the invocation of the functions. These functions respond to specific events. For example, the application developer can author a function that gets binary image data as the input and returns its compressed version. This function can be deployed as an independent 'unit of work and invoked with an image data to get the compressed version. This function would run in an isolated container managed by the cloud provider itself, and the application developer would only be busy with the parameter the cloud provider gets and the return data they give away. Obviously, this function alone does not make much sense, but cloud providers are also providing a mechanism to make these small functions respond to specific cloud events. For instance, you can configure this function to be invoked automatically whenever a new file is added to an S3 Bucket. In this way, this function will always be notified when there is a new image uploaded by your users and save a compressed version of it to another bucket. You can deploy another function that returns plain JSON objects that configure it to respond to HTTP requests via API Gateway. You would now have a fully scalable web service that you pay for as you go.

Sounds good? Then we warmly welcome you to the serverless computing world!

 For a good theoretical study on serverless computing, I recommend that you read Mike Robert's *Serverless Architectures*. He paints a big picture of the topic and carefully analyzes the advantage and drawbacks of a serverless approach. You can find information about this article in the bibliography section.

In this book, we will learn how to build a midsize serverless application with AWS Lambda and the Java language. Although Google Cloud Platform and Windows Azure offer similar functionalities, I picked AWS Lambda because, at the time of writing, AWS is the provider that offers the most mature solutions. I picked Java because, despite its power and popularity, I believe that Java has been always underestimated in the serverless computing community. In my opinion, this is because AWS started with offering JavaScript, thus the trend started with that language and went on with it. However, AWS Lambda has native support for Java, which offers a fully functional JVM 8 to developers. In this book, we will look at how to apply the most common techniques in the Java world, such as Dependency Injection, and try to apply OOP design patterns to our functions. Unlike JavaScript equivalents, our functions will be more sophisticated and we will create great build systems thanks to Gradle. Gradle is Maven like build tool which uses Groovy based language that you can build sophisticated build configurations.

In this journey, we will begin with the following:

- We will create a fully serverless forum application on the AWS platform.
- We will use Java 8 as language. Google's **Guice** will be our dependency injection framework.
- We will use AWS CloudFormation to deploy our application. We will write small Gradle tasks that will help us to have a painless deployment process. Gradle will also manage our dependencies.

 CloudFormation is an automated AWS tool for the provisioning of cloud resources. With CloudFormation, you can define your whole cloud platform using a single JSON file without having to deal with CLI or AWS Console and deploy your application with one command in any AWS account. It is a very strong tool and I advise against usage of any other method to build AWS-based applications. With CloudFormation, you can have a solid definition of your application that works everywhere in the same way. Besides the benefits of such solidity in the production environment, CloudFormation also lets us define our infrastructure as code, so we can leverage source control and observe the development of our infrastructure along with our code. Therefore, in this book, you will not find any CLI command or AWS Console screenshot, but will find CloudFormation template files.

- We will create only REST endpoints and test them using a rest-assured testing tool. We will not create any frontend as it is out of the scope of this book. For REST endpoints, we will use **API Gateway**. For some backend services, we will also develop some standalone Lambda functions that will respond to cloud events, such as S3 events.
- We will use **AWS S3** to store static files.
- We will use **DynamoDB** as the data layer and store static files in Amazon S3. For the search feature, we will learn how to use **AWS CloudSearch**. We will use **SQS (Simple Queue Service)** and **SNS (Simple Notification Service)** for some backend services.
- You can use any IDE you want. We will operate on CLI, mostly with Gradle commands that make the project totally IDE-agnostic.

You may think that there are many unknown words in this list, especially if you are not familiar with the AWS ecosystem. No worries! We expect you to be familiar only with the Java language and common patterns such as Dependency Injection. Knowledge of Gradle is a plus but not mandatory. We do not expect you to know about the services that AWS offers. We will be covering most details and referring to relevant documentation whenever needed, and after completing this book, you will know what these abbreviations mean. However, you are free to go to the AWS documentation and learn what those services are offering.

The forum application we will be implementing will be a very basic but over-engineered application. It will include the REST API that users can register, create topics and posts under existing topics, update their profiles, and do some other operations. The application will have some supporting services, such as sending mobile notifications to users when someone replies to their posts, an image resizer, and so on. As it is very typical web application and we are assuming that the audience of the book is already familiar with the business requirements of such an application, we are omitting the definition of all the systems at this stage. Instead, we will adopt an iterative agile methodology and define the specifications of these subsystems when we need them in the upcoming chapters.

In this chapter, we will cover the following topics:

- A brief theoretical introduction to AWS Lambda
- Setting up an AWS account
- Creating the Gradle project for our project and configuring dependencies
- Developing the base Lambda handler class that will be shared with all Lambda functions in the future
- Testing this implementation locally using Junit
- Creating and deploying a basic Lambda function
- Introducing AWS Lambda

As stated earlier, AWS Lambda is the core AWS offering we will be busy with throughout this book. While other services offer us important functionalities such as data storage, message queues, search, and so on, AWS Lambda is the glue that combines all this with our business logic.

In the simplest words, AWS Lambda is a computing service where we can upload our code, create independent functions, and tie them to specific events in the cloud infrastructure. AWS manages all the infrastructure where our functions run and performs all of the administration of the compute resources, including server and operating system maintenance, capacity provisioning and automatic scaling, code monitoring, and logging. When our function has high demand, AWS automatically increases the underlying machine count to ensure that our function performs with the same performance. AWS Lambda supports JavaScript (Node.js), Java, and Python languages natively.

You can write AWS Lambda functions in one of the languages supported natively. Regardless of the chosen language, there is a common pattern that includes the following core concepts:

- **Handler:** Handler is a method that Lambda runtime calls whenever your function is invoked. You configure the name of this method when you create your Lambda function. When your function is invoked, the Lambda runtime injects the event data to this method. After this entry point, your method can call other methods in your deployment package. In Java, the class that includes the handler method should implement a specific interface provided by the AWS Lambda Runtime dependency. We will look at the details later in this chapter.
- **Context:** A special context object is also passed to the handler method. Using this object, you can access some AWS Lambda runtime values, such as the request ID, the execution time remaining before AWS Lambda terminates your Lambda function, and so on.
- **Event:** Events are JSON payloads that Lambda runtime injects to your Lambda function upon execution. You can call Lambda function from many sources, like HTTP requests, messaging systems, and so on. For each execution type, structure of JSON will be different. In Node.js environment, events are passed to handler functions in string format. In Java runtime, you have two possibilities: Receive event as InputStream and parse yourself or create a POJO that can be deserialized from expected JSON. For the latter case, Lambda runtime will use Jackson library to convert the event to that POJO. In this book we will create our own deserializer because default Jackson configuration is not meeting our requirements.

- **Logging:** Within your Lambda function, you can log in to CloudWatch, which is the built-in logging feature offered by AWS. In this book, we will use log4j to generate log entries. We will then leverage the custom log4j appender offered by AWS to write our logs to CloudWatch.
- **Exceptions:** After successful execution, Lambda functions return a result in the JSON format. It is also possible to identify an execution error using Java exceptions. We will make heavy use of exceptions to tell to the AWS runtime about failed executions, and it will be especially useful in returning different HTTP code in our REST API.

AWS Lambda functions can be invoked manually or by responding to different events. They are normal functions: you give them an event object and you get the results. During the execution, Lambda functions are totally agnostic about who is calling them. However, invoking them manually does not make much sense. Instead, we configure them to respond to Cloud events. Invoking Lambda functions manually is useful when we test our functions for different type of inputs and we will actually do that when we test our functions manually. However, the real power of Lambda functions appears when their invocation is out of our control. In this book, we will configure AWS functions to respond to different cloud events. Here are examples of some of them:

- **REST Endpoints:** We will develop Lambda functions that will be asynchronously invoked by HTTP requests. We will be using API Gateway. This service accepts HTTP requests, converts the HTTP request parameters into the Lambda event that our function will understand, and finally converts the output of the Lambda to the desired JSON output. We will be creating three-four endpoints using this technology and have a fully scalable API for our application.

- **Resizing Images:** For the most of the use cases, we do not even need to develop a REST API for our needs. In this scenario, our users will upload their profile photos to **AWS S3**. We will not write a special endpoint for that; instead, client application will use **AWS Cognito** to temporarily obtain the IAM credentials that will only allow you to upload files to the S3 bucket. Once the image is uploaded, S3 will invoke our Lambda function and our function will resize the image and save it to the resized images bucket. After this point, the users will be able to access to resized images using the **CloudFront** CDN. In other words, we will have built an image service without using or developing any REST API endpoints:

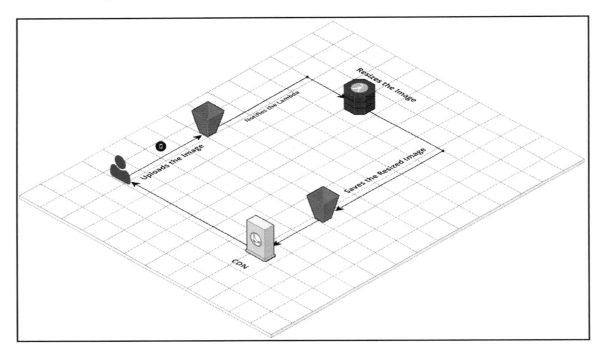

In the following chapters, you will understand much better how Lambda functions work with practical examples.

After this introduction, it is time to get our hands dirty and write some code.

Preparing the environment

Before we start digging into our project, we have to have an AWS account and the AWS CLI installed on our system. Even if you already have an AWS account, it is recommended that you open a new one because every new AWS account will come with a free tier available for 12 months following your AWS sign-up date. With the free tier, you will not have to pay for most of the resources we will install throughout the book. To set up a new account, perform the following steps:

1. Open `http://aws.amazon.com/` and then choose **Create an AWS Account**.
2. Follow the online instructions.

Once you create your account, you will have to create security credentials for yourself. **IAM (Identity and Access Management)** is a service where you manage the security configuration of your AWS account. Here, you can create more than one user and allow them granularly to specific cloud resources. For every user, you can create up to two security credentials that you can use to access AWS APIs via different SDKs or the AWS CLI tool.

When you sign up a new AWS account, a root user is created, but usage of this account with security credentials should be avoided. This account has unlimited access to your account, and if you expose your security credentials accidentally to the public domain, such as a public git repository, your account can be compromised. For the sake of simplicity, we will create a new IAM user with administrator access.

The Internet is full of stories of stolen AWS keys. It is known that some malicious software is scanning every commit published to GitHub and when they detect AWS credentials accidentally published to a public repository, they spin up lots of virtual machines using those credentials to mine Bitcoins or for other purposes. While they make money with that, the owner of the AWS account is faced with excessive bills. Therefore, you should be very protective about access keys. Do not share them with anyone and restrict the usage right of AWS users using IAM policies. The credentials of the user we create here will not be hardcoded in any code and will be merely used to configure the AWS CLI. Even though the risk of granting administrator access to this user is relatively low in this case, we recommend that you be aware of potential issues.

To create the user, perform the following steps:

1. Navigate to `https://console.aws.amazon.com/iam`.
2. In the navigation pane, choose **Users** and then choose **Create New Users.**
3. Type the user name for the user to be created. You can create up to five users at the same time, but we need only one for now.
4. Make sure that the **Generate an access key for each user** checkbox is selected.
5. Click on **Create**.
6. On the next screen, you will be given the security credentials of the user you just created. This is the only opportunity to view the credentials. If you do not save them, you will need to create new access keys for the user. That's why it's important to save the **Access Key ID** and **Secret Access Key** now.

The user you just created does not have any access to AWS resources. AWS users gain the right to access depending on the IAM policies attached to them. Now we will attach an **AdministratorAccess** policy to that. To accomplish that, perform the following steps:

1. In the **Users** section, click on the user that you created.
2. On **Permissions** tab, click on the **AttachPolicy** button.
3. Check the **AdministratorAccess** policy and click on the **Attach Policy** button in the bottom-right section.

We have completed creating a user with administrator rights.

Installing AWS CLI

We are going to proceed to installing **AWS CLI (Command Line Interface)**. The AWS CLI is a tool to manage your AWS services. It is very a powerful tool that can control all the AWS services and it is the preferred method for programmatic access to AWS APIs via the command line. Although we will use Gradle to control our deployment and the cloud resource creation process, it is useful to have the AWS CLI installed on our system.

Prerequisites

- Linux, OS X, or Unix
- Python 2 version 2.6.5+ or Python 3 version 3.3+

For Mac OS X and Linux, these three commands will install the AWS CLI on your system:

```
$ curl "https://s3.amazonaws.com/aws-cli/awscli-bundle.zip" -o
  "awscli-bundle.zip"
$ unzip awscli-bundle.zip
$ sudo ./awscli-bundle/install -i /usr/local/aws -b /usr/local/bin/aws
```

Once you have the AWS CLI installed, you can configure it with the security credentials you obtained previously. Type `aws configure` and follow the instructions. After you complete this step, your credentials will be saved at `~/.aws/configure` and different programming platform SD's and the AWS CLI tool will use these credentials when they invoke AWS APIs.

Gradle

We must also have Gradle installed on our system. Gradle is a modern build tool that got popularity with Android. It uses Groovy-based DSL instead of XML files and mixes declarative and imperative type of build configuration. With Gradle you can define dependencies and project properties, and also you can write functions. We will leverage Gradle to build our deployment system, so with only one command we will be able to deploy all our software to cloud.

Throughout the book, we will use the Gradle wrapper that locks the Gradle version for the project, thus providing integrity between different teams. However, in order to run the gradle wrapper task, which will create the gradle wrapper files in our project, we have to have at least one Gradle version locally in our system.

If you do not have it already, execute the following:

```
$ curl -s https://get.sdkman.io | bash
```

Then, open a new terminal and type this:

```
$ sdk install gradle 2.14
```

This will install the Gradle 2.14 version.

Creating the project

Finally, we can start creating our project. We will create our project in our home directory, so we can start with these commands:

```
$ mkdir -p ~ /serverlessbook
$ cd ~/serverlessbook
```

Once we create the working directory, we can create the `build.gradle` file, which will be the main build file of our project:

```
$ touch build.gradle
```

We can start with the Gradle wrapper task, which will generate Gradle files in our project. Write this block into the `build.gradle` file:

```
task wrapper(type: Wrapper) {
  gradleVersion = '2.14'
}
```

And then execute the command:

```
$ gradle wrapper
```

This will create Gradle wrapper files in our project. This means that in the root directory of the project, `./gradlew` can be called instead of the local gradle. It is a nice feature of Gradle: Let's assume that you distributed your project to other team members and you are not sure whether they have Gradle installed on their system (or its version if they already have). With the Gradle wrapper, you make sure that everybody who checked out the project will run Gradle 2.14 if they run `./gradlew`. If they do not have any Gradle version in their system, the script will download it.

We can now proceed to add the declarations needed for all projects. Add this code block to the `build.gradle` file:

```
// allprojects means this configuration
// will be inherited by the root project itself and subprojects
allprojects {
    // Artifact Id of the projct
```

```
group 'com.serverlessbook'
// Version of the project
version '1.0'
// Gradle JAVA plugin needed for JAVA support
apply plugin: 'java'
// We will be using JAVA 8, then 1.8
sourceCompatibility = 1.8
}
```

With this code block, we tell to Gradle that we are building a Java 8 project with the artifact ID com.serverlessbook and version 1.0.

Also, we need to create the settings.gradle file, which will include some generic settings about the project and subproject names in the future. In the root project, create a new file with the name settings.gradle and type this line:

```
rootProject.name = 'forum'
```

Actually, this line is optional. When the root project name is not given a name explicitly, Gradle assigns the name of the directory where the project is placed as the project name. For consistency, however, it is a good idea to name the project explicitly because other developers may always check out our code to a directory with another name and we would not love that our project has another name then.

 In our Gradle build script, we get access to important values about the project with variables such as project.name and project.version.

Now we should add repositories to fetch the dependencies for the project itself and the build script. In order to accomplish this, first, we have to add this block to the build.gradle file:

```
allprojects {
  repositories {
    mavenCentral()
    jcenter()
    maven {
      url "https://jitpack.io"
    }
  }
}
```

Here, we defined Maven Central, Bintray JCenter, and Jitpack as the three most popular repositories. We need the same dependencies for the build script, thus we add the following block to the same file:

```
buildscript {
  repositories {
    mavenCentral()
    jcenter()
    maven {
        url "https://jitpack.io"
    }
  }
}
```

 Repositories and dependencies defined in buildscript are used only in the Gradle build script itself. We will excessively use build script dependencies because our Gradle script will manage the deployment process. Therefore, it is important that you have these repositories for the build script as well.

Implementing the Lambda Dependency

In the previous section, we already finished the generic Gradle setup. In this section, we will learn how to write Lambda functions and create the very core part of our project that will be the entry point for all our Lambda functions.

In our project, we will have more than one specific AWS Lambda function, one for each REST endpoint and several more for auxiliary services. These functions will share some common code and dependencies; therefore, is convenient to create a subproject under our root project. In Gradle, subprojects act like different projects but they can inherit the build configuration from their root project. In any case, these projects will be compiled independently and produce different JAR files in their respective build directories.

In our project structure, one subproject will include the common code we will need for every single Lambda function, and this project will be required as a dependency by other subprojects that implement the Lambda function. As a naming convention, the core Lambda subproject will be called lambda, while the individual Lambda function that will be deployed will be named by the lambda- prefix.

We can start implementing this core AWS Lambda subproject and create a new directory under our root directory called with the its name:

```
$ mkdir lambda
```

Then, let's create a new `build. gradle` file for the newly created subproject:

```
$ touch lambda/build.gradle
```

By default, Gradle will not recognize the new subproject just because we created a new directory under the root directory. To make Gradle recognize it as a subproject, we must add a new include directive to the `settings.gradle` file. This command will add the new line to `settings.gradle`:

```
$ echo $"include 'lambda'" >> settings.gradle
```

After this point, our subproject can inherit the directives from the root project so we will not have to repeat the most of those.

Now we can define the required dependencies for our main Lambda library. At this point, we will need only the `aws-lambda-java-core` and `jackson-databind` packages. While the former is the standard AWS library for Lambda functions, the latter is used for JSON serialization and deserialization purposes, which we will be using heavily. In order to add these dependencies, just add these lines in the `lambda/build.gradle` file:

```
dependencies {
    compile 'com.amazonaws:aws-lambda-java-core:1.1.0'
    compile 'com.fasterxml.jackson.core:jackson-databind:2.6.+'
}
```

Previously, we mentioned that AWS Lambda is invoking a specific method for every Lambda function to inject the event data and accept this method's response as the Lambda response. To determine which method to invoke, AWS Lambda leverages interfaces. `aws-lambda-java core` includes the `RequestStreamHandler` interface in the `com.amazonaws.services.lambda.runtime` package. In our base Lambda package, we will create a method that implements this interface.

Now let's create our first package and implement the `LambdaHandler<I, O>` method inside it:

```
$ mkdir -p lambda/src/main/java/com/serverlessbook/lambda
$ touch lambda/src/main/java/com/serverlessbook/lambda/
    LambdaHandler.java
```

Let's start implementing our class:

```
package com.serverlessbook.lambda;

import com.fasterxml.jackson.databind.ObjectMapper;
import com.amazonaws.services.lambda.runtime.Context;
import com.amazonaws.services.lambda.runtime.RequestStreamHandler;
```

```
import java.io.IOException;
import java.io.InputStream;
import java.io.OutputStream;
import java.lang.reflect.ParameterizedType;

public abstract class LambdaHandler<I, O> implements RequestStreamHandler {

    @Override
    public void handleRequest(InputStream input, OutputStream output,
      Context context) throws IOException {
    }

    public abstract O handleRequest(I input, Context context);
}
```

As you may have noted, this class is using generics. It is expected that the implemented handleRequest abstract method in the inheriting classes accept one **POJO (Plain Old Java Object)** and return another POJO. On the other hand, in the overridden handleRequest method gets AWS Lambda event data as InputStream and it should return OutputStream including the output JSON. Our base LambdaHandler method will implement methods that convert JSON into InputStream and OutputStream into JSON. The I and O type references are the key points in this case because using this information, our base class will know which POJO classes it should use when it carries out the transformation.

 If you have ever read the AWS Lambda documentation, you might have seen the RequestHandler class in the AWS Lambda library, which exactly does what we will do in the base class. However, Lambda's built-in JSON serialization does not meet the requirements for our project because it does not support advanced features of the Jackson JSON library. That's why we are implementing our own JSON serializer. If you are building a simple Lambda function that does not require these advanced options, you can check out https://docs.aws.amazon.com/lambda/latest/dg/java-handler-io-type-pojo.htmland use the built-in serializer.

Before we go on implementing the base Lambda handler method, I suggest that you look at the **TDD (Test Driven Development)** approach and write a test class for the planned implementation. Having the test class will explain better which type of implementation we need and will draw a clear picture about the next step.

Before we start implementing the test, first, we have to add Junit as a dependency to our project. Open `build.gradle` in the root project and add these files to the end:

```
allprojects {
  dependencies {
    testCompile group: 'junit', name: 'junit', version: '4.11'
  }
}
```

Then, let's create our first test file:

```
$ mkdir -p lambda/src/test/java/com/serverlessbook/lambda
$ touch lambda/src/test/java/com/serverlessbook/lambda/
  LambdaHandlerTest.java
```

We can then to start implementing it writing the following code to `LambdaHandlerTest` file we've just created. First of all, inside the test class we will create two stub POJO's and a `LambdaHandler` class to run the test against:

```
public class LambdaHandlerTest {
  protected static class TestInput {
    public String value;
  }
  protected static class TestOutput {
    public String value;
  }
  protected static class TestLambdaHandler extends LambdaHandler<TestInput,
    TestOutput> {
    @Override
    public TestOutput handleRequest(TestInput input, Context context) {
      TestOutput testOutput = new TestOutput();
      testOutput.value = input.value;
      return testOutput;
    }
  }
}
```

Here, we have the sample `TestInput` and `TestOutput` classes, which are simple POJO classes with one variable each and one `TestLambdaHandler` class that implements the `LambdaHandler` class with type references to these POJO classes. As you may have noted, the stub class does not do too much and simply returns a `TestOutput` object with the same value it gets.

Finally, we can add the test method that will exactly emulate the AWS Lambda runtime and carry out a black-box text over our TestLambdaHandler method:

```
@Test
public void handleRequest() throws Exception {
    String jsonInputAndExpectedOutput = "{\"value\":\"testValue\"}";
    InputStream exampleInputStream = new
      ByteArrayInputStream(jsonInputAndExpectedOutput.getBytes(
      StandardCharsets.UTF_8));
    OutputStream exampleOutputStream = new OutputStream() {
      private final StringBuilder stringBuilder = new StringBuilder();

      @Override
      public void write(int b) {
          stringBuilder.append((char) b);
      }

      @Override
      public String toString() {
        return stringBuilder.toString();
      }
    };

    TestLambdaHandler lambdaHandler = new TestLambdaHandler();
    lambdaHandler.handleRequest(exampleInputStream, exampleOutputStream,
null);
    assertEquals(jsonInputAndExpectedOutput, exampleOutputStream.toString());
}
```

To run the test, we can execute this command:

```
$ ./gradlew test
```

Once you run the command, you will see that test will fail. It is normal for our test to fail because we did not complete the implementation of our LambdaHandler method and this is how Test Driven Development works: first, write the test, and then implement it until the test returns to green.

I think it is time to move on to implementation. Open the `LambdaHandler` class again and add a field with Jackson's `ObjectMapper` type and create the default constructor to initiate this object. You can add the following code to beginning of the class:

```
final ObjectMapper mapper;

protected LambdaHandler() {
    mapper = new ObjectMapper();
}
```

 AWS Lambda does not create an object from the handler class for every new request. Instead, it creates an instance of the class for the first request (called the 'heat up' stage) and uses the same instance for other requests. This created object will stay in the memory for about 20 minutes if there is no consequent request for that Lambda function. It is good to know about this undocumented fact because it means that we can cache objects among different requests using object properties, like we do here for `ObjectMapper`. In this case `ObjectMapper` will not be created for every request, and it will be 'cached' in the memory. However, you can think of the handler object like Servlets and you should pay attention to thread safety before you decide to use object properties.

Now we need helper methods in the handler for serialization and deserialization. First, we need a method to get the `Class` object for the `I` type reference:

```
@SuppressWarnings("unchecked")
private Class<I> getInputType() {
  return (Class<I>) ((ParameterizedType)
    getClass().getGenericSuperclass()).getActualTypeArguments()[0];
}
```

We can use the deserializer and serializer methods:

```
private I deserializeEventJson(InputStream inputStream, Class<I> clazz)
throws
  IOException {
  return mapper.readerFor(clazz).readValue(inputStream);
}

private void serializeOutput(OutputStream outputStream, O output) throws
  IOException {
    mapper.writer().writeValue(outputStream, output);
}
```

Finally, we can implement the handler method:

```
@Override
public void handleRequest(InputStream input, OutputStream output,
    Context context) throws IOException {
    I inputObject = deserializeEventJson(input, getInputType());
    O handlerResult = handleRequest(inputObject, context);
    serializeOutput(output, handlerResult);
}
```

It seems we are good to go. Let's run the test again:

```
$ ./gradlew test
```

Congratulations! We completed an important step and built the base class for our Lambda functions.

Hello Lambda!

We are now ready to implement our first Lambda function, which will just upload to the cloud via AWS CLI and invoke manually.

First, we have to create a new subproject, like we did earlier. This time, the subproject will be called `lambda-test`. We can easily do that with these two commands:

```
$ mkdir -p lambda-test/src/main/java/com/serverlessbook/lambda/test
$ echo $"include 'lambda'" >> settings.gradle
$ touch lambda-test/src/main/java/com/serverlessbook/lambda/
  test/Handler.java
```

We can create a blank class in `Handler.java` like this:

```
package com.serverlessbook.lambda.test;
public class Handler {}
```

Note that we've already chosen a naming convention for package naming: while our base Lambda package sits in the `com.serverlessbook.lambda` package, individual Lambda functions are in packages named with the `com.serverlessbook.lambda.{function-name}` format. We will also call handler classes `Handler` because it sounds perfect in English: `Handler` implements `LambdaHandler`. This naming convention is, of course, up to you and your team, but it is convenient to keep things organized.

If you are already familiar with the Gradle build mechanism, you might have realized that before we proceed to implement Lambda's handler function, we have to add the `lambda` subproject to `lambda-test` as a dependency, and that is a very valid point. The easiest way to do that would be by creating a `build.gradle` file for the `lambda-test` subproject, add the dependency in the `dependencies {}` block, and move on. On the other hand, we know that our project will include more than one Lambda function, and all of them will share the same build configuration. Putting this configuration in a central location is a very good idea for clear organization and maintainability. Fortunately, Gradle is a very powerful tool that allows such scenarios. We can create a build configuration block in our root project and apply this configuration only to subprojects whose name starts with `lambda-`, in accordance with our subproject naming convention. Then, we can edit our root `build.gradle` and add this block to the end of the file:

```
configure(subprojects.findAll()) {
  if (it.name.startsWith("lambda-")) {
  }
}
```

It tells Gradle to apply this configuration only to Lambda projects. Inside this block, we will have an important configuration, but for now, we can start with the most important dependency and edit the block to appear like this:

```
configure(subprojects.findAll()) {
  if (it.name.startsWith("lambda-")) {
    dependencies {
      compile project(':lambda')
    }
  }
}
```

In this step, we have to add another important build configuration, which is the **Shadow plugin**. The Shadow plugin creates an uber-JAR (also known as a fat JAR or JAR with dependencies) that is required by AWS Lambda. After each build phase, this plugin will compile all the dependencies along with that project's source into a second-and-bigger-JAR file, which will be our deployment package for AWS Lambda. To install this plugin, first, we have to edit the `buildscript` configuration of the root `build.gradle` file. After editing, the `buildscript` section should look like this:

```
buildscript {
  repositories {
    mavenCentral()
    jcenter()
    maven {
      url "https://jitpack.io"
    }
```

```
    }

    dependencies {
      classpath "com.github.jengelman.gradle.plugins:shadow:1.2.3"
    }
}
```

We have to apply the plugin to all lambda functions. We have to add two lines to the lambda subproject's configuration, and the final version should look like this:

```
configure(subprojects.findAll()) {
    if (it.name.startsWith("lambda-")) {
        dependencies {
            compile project(':lambda')
        }

        apply plugin: "com.github.johnrengelman.shadow"
        build.finalizedBy shadowJar
    }
}
```

The first line applies the Shadow plugin, which adds `shadowJar` task to every lambda subproject. The second directive ensures that after every `build` task, the `shadowJar` is automatically executed, thus an uber-JAR is placed into the build directory.

You can try our basic build configuration by running this command in the root directory:

```
$ ./gradlew build
```

You can see the uber-JAR file `lambda-test-1.0-all.jar` in the `lambada-test/build/libs` directory.

Now we are going to implement the handler function with very basic functionality, like what we did previously to test the base handler. For the sake of simplicity, we will define input and output classes as inner static classes, although this is not the recommended way of creating classes in Java. Now open the Handler class and edit it like this:

```
package com.serverlessbook.lambda.test;

import com.amazonaws.services.lambda.runtime.Context;
import com.serverlessbook.lambda.LambdaHandler;

public class Handler extends LambdaHandler<Handler.TestInput,
Handler.TestOutput> {
    static class TestInput {
        public String value;
    }
```

```
static class TestOutput {
    public String value;
}
@Override
public TestOutput handleRequest(TestInput input, Context context) {
    TestOutput testOutput = new TestOutput();
    testOutput.value = input.value;
    return testOutput;
}
}
```

That's it; we have now a very basic Lambda function, which is ready to deploy to the cloud. In the next section, we will deploy and run it on AWS Lambda runtime.

Deploying to the Cloud

Approaching the end of this chapter, we have a latest step, which is deploying our code to the cloud. In the next chapters, we will learn how to use CloudFormation for a production-ready deployment process. However, nothing is preventing us from using CLI to play a bit with Lambda at this stage.

Previously, we mentioned that AWS resources are protected by IAM policies and created a user and attached a policy to it. IAM has another entity type, which is called a role. Roles are very similar to users, and they are also identities and can access resources that are allowed by policies attached to them. However, while a user is associated with one person, roles can be assumed by whoever needs them. Lambda functions use roles to access other AWS resources. Every Lambda function should be associated with a role (execution role), and the Lambda function can call any resource that the policies attached to that role allow.

In the following chapters, while we create our CloudFormation stack, we will create very advanced role definitions. However, at this stage, our test Lambda function does not need to access any AWS resources; thus, a basic role with minimum access rights will be sufficient to run the example. In this section, you create an IAM role using the following predefined role type and access policy:

- The AWS service role of the AWS Lambda type. This role grants AWS Lambda permission to assume the role.
- The **AWSLambdaBasicExecutionRole** access policy that you attach to the role. This managed policy grants permissions for **Amazon CloudWatch** actions that your Lambda function needs for logging and monitoring.

To create the IAM role:

1. Sign in to the **Identity and Access Management (IAM)** console at `https://conso le.aws.amazon.com/iam/`.
2. In the navigation pane, choose **Roles** and then choose **Create New Role.**
3. Enter a role name, say, `lambda-execution-role`, and then choose **Next Step**.
4. On the next screen, select **AWS Lambda** in the **AWS Service Roles** section.
5. In **Attach Policy**, choose **AWSLambdaBasicExecutionRole** and then proceed.
6. Take down the **ARN** of the role you just created.

Now we are ready to deploy our first Lambda function. First, let's build our project again using the build command:

```
$ ./gradlew build
```

Check whether the uber-JAR file is created in the build folder. Then, create the function using AWS CLI:

```
$ aws lambda create-function \
  --region us-east-1\
  --function-name book-test \
  --runtime java8 \
  --role ROLE_ARN_YOU_CREATED \
  --handler com.serverlessbook.lambda.test.Handler \
  --zip-file fileb://${PWD}/lambda-test/build/libs/
    lambda-test-1.0-all.jar
```

If everything goes well, the following happens:

```
{
    "CodeSha256": "6cSUk4g8GdlhvApF6LfpT1dCOgemO2LOtrH7pZ6OATk=",
    "FunctionName": "book-test",
    "CodeSize": 1481805,
    "MemorySize": 128,
    "FunctionArn": "arn:aws:lambda:us-east-1:YOUR_ACCOUNT_ID:
      function:book-test",
    "Version": "$LATEST",
    "Role": "arn:aws:iam::YOUR_ACCOUNT-ID:role/lambda-execution-role",
    "Timeout": 3,
    "LastModified": "2016-08-22T22:12:30.419+0000",
    "Handler": "com.serverlessbook.lambda.test.Handler",
    "Runtime": "java8",
    "Description": ""
}
```

This means that your function has already been created. You can navigate to `https://eu-c entral-1.console.aws.amazon.com/lambda`to check whether your function is already there or not. To execute the function, you can use the following command:

```
$ aws lambda invoke --invocation-type RequestResponse \
                    --region us-east-1 \
                    --profile serverlessbook \
                    --function-name book-test \
                    --payload '{"value":"test"}' \
                    --log-type Tail \
                    /tmp/test.txt
```

You can see the output value in the `/tmp/test.txt` file and try the command with different values to see different outputs. Note that the first invocation is always slower, while the subsequent calls are significantly faster. This is because of the heat-up mechanism of AWS Lambda that we will mention later in the book.

Congratulations, and welcome to the world of AWS Lambda officially!

Summary

In this chapter, we described serverless computing and learned about the use cases in which it can be useful. We set up an AWS Account, created a skeleton Gradle project for our book, and wrote a basic library. Finally, we implemented a very basic Lambda function on top of our work and deployed and executed it.

In the next chapter, we will learn how to use Cloudformation for a more automatized deployment process and add the dependency injection framework to our project, which will orchestrate the different services we will implement in our project.

Bibliography

1. Amazon Web Services, *AWS S3 Pricing*, 16-8-2016. [Online]. Available: `https://a ws.amazon.com/s3/reduced-redundancy/`.
2. M. Roberts, *Serverless Architectures*, 04-08-2016. [Online]. Available: `http://marti nfowler.com/articles/serverless.html`. [Accessed 17 08 2016].

2
Infrastructure as a Code

In the previous chapter, we looked at the basics of AWS Lambda, starting with creating an AWS account to develop our first micro function. However, our deployment process was pretty manual and obviously not production-ready. Based on the principle of "if you repeat a task three times, it's time to automate", it is time to automate this process in order to build a first-class deployment process that will automate and facilitate our workflow.

If you have ever used AWS Lambda in other languages, you might have heard about some frameworks such as Serverless, Apex, or Kappa. These are valuable open source tools with great features, and they used to be very essential for AWS Lambda development with features such as packaging the code, creation of API Gateway endpoints, and so on. If you are authoring Lambda functions in JavaScript or Python, it is recommended that you leverage one of these frameworks. However, in the Java platform, we have already been using strong build tools, such as Maven or Gradle. If you are a Java person, with Gradle, we get rid of the complication of the build process and packaging artifacts. After we compile our code to a single fat JAR file, the next step would be to create AWS Lambda functions using them and create the API Gateway resources and methods. Until a few months ago, the mentioned tools were the easiest way to create these cloud resources, but with the latest developments of AWS, we do not need these tools anymore: CloudFormation is the default offering from AWS that meets all the requirements. At the end of the day, just using Gradle and CloudFormation, we can create our handcrafted automated build mechanism for any Serverless application.

Some of my colleagues have been criticizing me because I am ignoring the open source frameworks and reinventing the wheel with a custom build mechanism. This is a pretty subjective topic, and everybody may have a different option. If we can develop our own build system easily, as we are going to see in this chapter, I do not see any benefit of depending on a third-party tool and inheriting their complexity and possible problems. For Java, I prefer pure Java solutions, and at the moment, I want to teach you how we can deploy to AWS without the aid of third-party tools. I believe that in this way, you are going to learn about the internals of AWS more deeply

In this chapter, we will meet with CloudFormation, the legendary tool of AWS that automates the cloud resources with JSON templates. CloudFormation will be one of the main tools we will use in this book, and it is maybe the most important AWS tool ever. I personally believe that.

In this journey, first, we will extend our build phase and add a functionality to our Gradle build script to upload compiled JAR files to AWS S3 storage. Once we have our artifacts in the cloud, the Gradle build script will install our handcrafted CloudFormation template to our AWS account. At the end of the chapter, we will have a single command to rule all. It will execute all the tests, build the artifacts, upload them to the cloud, and finally, deploy our application.

CloudFormation may seem a bit complicated in the beginning, but we will try to explain the concepts as clearly as possible and refer to the relevant documentation as much as possible.

We will cover the following topics in this chapter:

- Uploading the artifacts to cloud
- Infrastructure as code with CloudFormation
- Deploying our first Lambda with CloudFormation

Uploading the artifacts to Cloud

In the previous chapter, we deployed our first Lambda function via the AWS CLI. As you remember, we used the locally stored JAR file in the command line, and we saw that having the JAR file on our development machine works for such a simple scenario. However, when we want to deploy our Lambda functions via CloudFormation, we have to upload the very same JAR file to an S3 storage. S3 is the oldest and maybe the most famous AWS offering and provides a scalable and durable storage area for developers. In S3, you can store any type of files and pay only for the storage you actually use. In this chapter, we will introduce S3 to upload our artifacts, but in the following chapters, we will also use it to store uploaded files by users, such as profile pictures.

As a first step toward automated deployment, we will use the AWS Gradle plugin built by Classmethod Inc. This is a set of plugin that allows access to AWS API's directly from Gradle code. Detailed documentation can be found at `https://github.com/classmethod/gradle-aws-plugin`. The plugin has support for a couple of AWS services, but for now, we are going to use only S3 and CloudFormation support. Let's start with adding the plugin definition and some generic configuration to our `build.gradle` file. First, add the plugin to the classpath of buildscript:

```
buildscript {
  repositories {
    .....
  }
  dependencies
  {
    classpath "com.github.jengelman.gradle.plugins:shadow:1.2.3"
    classpath "jp.classmethod.aws:gradle-aws-plugin:0.+"
  }
}
```

Then, just below this block, let's add this block to apply the plugin to the root project and all the subprojects:

```
allprojects {
  apply plugin: "jp.classmethod.aws"
  aws {
    region = "us-east-1"
  }
}
```

Here, we picked `us-east-1` (North Virginia) as the region, but you can select another region depending on the location of your clients. This means that all our applications will be deployed to the us-east-1 region.

This is a citation of the AWS documentation: the AWS Cloud infrastructure is built around regions and **availability zones (AZs)**. A region is a physical location in the world where we have multiple availability zones. Availability zones consist of one or more discrete data centers, each with redundant power, networking and connectivity, housed in separate facilities. These availability zones offer you the ability to operate production applications and databases, which are more highly available, fault-tolerant, and scalable than would be possible from a single data center.

Every region has a different set of services. For the service availability list per region, check out `https://aws.amazon.com/about-aws/global-infr astructure/regional-product-services/`. At the time of writing, the us-east-1 (North Virginia), us-west-2 (Oregon), eu-west-1 (Ireland), and ap-northeast-1 (Tokyo) regions are supporting all the services we are going to use throughout the book.

After the generic configuration, the first AWS-related task that we are going to create will be the automated creation of an S3 bucket. We will use this S3 bucket to upload the created artifacts and the CloudFormation template. Our gradle script will first upload the shadow JAR files to the S3 bucket for every Lambda function. Then, in the final stage, the CloudFormation template will be uploaded to the same bucket. As the last step, the Gradle script will trigger the creation or update of the CloudFormation template in AWS. AWS will read the JSON configuration, create the desired resources (IAM roles, Lambda functions, and so on). When we define our Lambda function in the CloudFormation template, we will refer to the JAR file location in the deployment bucket and AWS will automatically fetch the JAR from there in order to create the Lambda function. So first, we will create this essential task to create the deployment bucket if it does not exist. In the `build.gradle` file, let's add this snippet just before the `configure (subprojects.findAll {` `it.name.startsWith("lambda-") })` part:

```
def deploymentBucketName = "serverless-book-${aws.region}"
def deploymentTime = new
java.text.SimpleDateFormat("yyyyMMddHHmmss").format(new Date());

allprojects {
    apply plugin: "jp.classmethod.aws.s3"
    task createDeploymentBucket(type:
jp.classmethod.aws.gradle.s3.CreateBucketTask) {
```

```
        bucketName deploymentBucketName
        ifNotExists true
    }
}

configure(subprojects.findAll()) {
    if (it.name.startsWith("lambda-")) {
    ......
```

Here, you might have noticed that we created two global variables. The first one is the name of the deployment bucket. We suffix the bucket name for every region using the `${aws.region}` variable that we previously set in the AWS plugin configuration.

For your project, you should change the bucket name with a unique name because, in AWS S3, bucket names are global and they must be unique. If you copy and paste the code snippet directly, you will see that the bucket creation will fail because a bucket with the name in the example code is already existing.

Now you can run the `./gradlew createDeploymentBucket` command to see whether your task is working. After running the command, you can check the bucket using AWS CLI with the following command:

```
$ aws s3 ls
```

You should see `serverless-book-us-east-1` in the list on the screen.

Now we have to extend the build phase of Lambda subprojects. As you may remember from the previous chapter, we created a block to write the build script only for subprojects starting with the `lambda-` prefix. Now, in this block, just after the `build.finalizedBy shadowJar` line, let's add this block:

```
    def producedJarFilePath = it.tasks.shadowJar.archivePath
    def s3Key = "artifacts/${it.name}/${it.version}/${deploymentTime}.jar"

    task uploadArtifactsToS3(type:
    jp.classmethod.aws.gradle.s3.AmazonS3FileUploadTask,
      dependsOn: [build, createDeploymentBucket]) {
      bucketName deploymentBucketName
      file producedJarFilePath
      key s3Key
    }
```

Here, we created a new task, which uploads the shadow JAR to the S3 bucket. Note that the s3Key variable is changing every time we run the Gradle script, so a new file will always be uploaded to S3. This is important because in the following sections, we will inject the deploymentTime variable to CloudFormation, and thus AWS will always fetch the latest version of the JAR file and update the Lambda function. Also, note that uploadArtifactsToS3 depends on the build and createDeploymentBucket tasks. Also, we access the created JAR file's path as an object by the it.tasks.shadowJar.archivePath variable. This is a variable created automatically by the Shadow JAR plugin, and it returns a file object pointing to a shadow JAR file in the build library. Now we can run the newly created task to see it in action. Run this command on the root directory:

```
$ ./gradlew uploadArtifactsToS3
```

Thanks to Gradle's task dependency feature, this command will automatically trigger and build the S3 bucket creation tasks before itself, and as you can see in the output, the test, build, shadowJar, S3 bucket creation tasks will be executed before the upload tasks come into action and upload the JAR file to the S3 file. For now, we have only one Lambda function project (lambda-test), so this task will run only once, but when we add more Lambda functions, this task will be propagated to other Lambda functions as well, so any change will be automatically reflected to the subprojects. Now we can check whether the artifact is uploaded to S3 via AWS CLI:

```
$ aws s3 ls s3://serverless-book-us-east-1/artifacts/lambda-test/1.0/
```

Don't forget to change the bucket name with your bucket name to see the result. In the output, you should see the uploaded JAR file by our task.

So far, so good. We solved the packaging issue using Gradle and without any other third-party tools. Now things are getting harder. In the next section, we will create our first CloudFormation template to deploy our JAR to AWS Lambda.

Infrastructure as Code with CloudFormation

Starting from this section, we will learn how to use a very important AWS tool, CloudFormation. AWS resources mostly have complicated and countless options, and provisioning them manually using AWS Console is not always a good option because this manual process may cause an issue because of a misconfiguration or forgotten option; also, the provisioning process would not be reproducible. Assume that you have to migrate the whole application to another AWS account or you want to remove and create everything from scratch. Creating BASH scripts with AWS CLI commands might be another option, but it would not solve some of the problems mentioned earlier; for example, deleting the whole application or changing some of the configuration in our stack would need refactoring of the BASH script or finding and removing the resources belonging to your application.

With CloudFormation, you can create a JSON (alternatively, a YAML) file that declares all the resources your application will use, relate the resources between them, and deploy, update, or delete the whole stack in one click. With CloudFormation, you also do not need to figure out the order of provisioning of different resources if some of them are depending on others. CloudFormation will calculate the dependencies between different resources and will reorder their provisioning.

CloudFormation is a very detailed topic through which we can only cover the relevant parts of our project. While authoring your templates, you will always need to refer to the documentation to see the available options for every resource type (`https://docs.aws.amazon.com/AWSCloudFormation/latest/UserGuide`).

To get started, we can create an example template in any directory and deploy it. Now create a text file with the name `cloudformation.test.template` and write this snippet into it:

```
{
  "Resources": {
    "DeploymentBucket": {
      "Type": "AWS::S3::Bucket",
      "Properties": {
        "AccessControl": "PublicRead"
      }
    }
  }
}
```

This template is very straightforward. It basically creates an S3 bucket with the `PublicRead` permission. The template does not specify any other properties, so AWS will use the default ones. Now let's look at the template in action. In the directory where you created the template file, execute this command:

```
$ aws cloudformation create-stack --region us-east-1 --stack-name
    test-stack --template-body file://${PWD}/cloudformation.test.template
```

This command will return stack ID. You can now navigate to AWS Console's CloudFormation section in the `us-east-1` region and check out the progress. (You can find the console at
`https://eu-west-1.console.aws.amazon.com/cloudformation/home?region=us-east-1`.)

Once the CloudFormation stack is deployed, you can see the CREATE_COMPLETE text on the status field of your stack. Now execute this command to see the S3 bucket created by your template:

```
$ aws s3 ls
```

Among the buckets, you can see a bucket with the name `test-start-deploymentbucket-RANDOM_ID`. The random ID is generated by CloudFormation and appended to the resource name. It is possible to override these random names, but if you are installing the same template more than once to the same account, it is a good practice to leave it as is in order to prevent any collision between different stack resources.

Now let's look at how we can update the stack. Let's assume that we want to update the website configuration of our bucket. Now we can update the template file like this:

```json
{
    "Resources": {
        "DeploymentBucket": {
            "Type": "AWS::S3::Bucket",
            "Properties": {
                "AccessControl": "PublicRead",
                "WebsiteConfiguration" : {
                    "IndexDocument" : "index.html",
                    "ErrorDocument" : "error.html"
                }
            }
        }
    }
}
```

As you can see, we added a new attribute to the bucket. Now let's execute the following command:

```
$ aws cloudformation update-stack --region us-east-1
  --stack-name test-stack --template-body
  file://${PWD}/cloudformation.test.template
```

AWS will return the stack ID again, but this time, it will return the existing one and perform the changes to keep the stack up to date with the template. After the update completes, you can navigate to the S3 console to verify that your bucket has the configuration you specified in the template file.

As a last step, we can delete the stack, along with all its resources, with only one command:

```
$ aws cloudformation delete-stack --region eu-west-1
  --stack-name test-stack
```

This will clean up your stack.

The default behavior of removing a stack is to delete all the resources. But sometimes, especially when your resource has data, you might prefer to leave the resource even if the stack is deleted. Adding "DeletionPolicy": "Retain" to the resource will prevent AWS from deleting the resource when the CloudFormation stack is deleted.

Deploying our first Lambda with CloudFormation

In this section, we will create our first template and deploy the stack using our Gradle script. We can start writing our template by creating a text file named `cloudformation.template` in the root directory of our project:

```
$ cd ~/serverlessbook
$ touch cloudformation.template
```

In this section, we will be defining three CloudFormation resources:

- The IAM role
- A custom IAM policy to be attached to the role created earlier
- A Lambda function

For the first resource, we can start with IAM Role, which our Lambda function will use for execution. In the first chapter, we briefly looked at what an IAM Role is. Let's assume that our Lambda function will access S3 buckets in our accounts. How we can allow our Lambda function to access S3 buckets as read-only but prevent it from writing to buckets? These permissions are configured via IAM Roles. When the AWS Lambda function is executed, it takes temporary AWS credentials belonging to an IAM Role, which you configure when you create the Lambda function. The permissions you give to that IAM Role can be then used by the Lambda function. We can first start with writing this snippet in our first CloudFormation template:

```json
{
  "Resources": {
    "LambdaExecutionRole": {
      "Type": "AWS::IAM::Role",
      "Properties": {
        "Path": "/",
        "AssumeRolePolicyDocument": {
          "Version": "2012-10-17",
          "Statement": [
            {
              "Effect": "Allow",
              "Principal": {
                "Service": [
                  "lambda.amazonaws.com"
                ]
              },
              "Action": [
                "sts:AssumeRole"
              ]
            }
          ]
        },
        "ManagedPolicyArns": [
          "arn:aws:iam::aws:policy/service-role/
            AWSLambdaVPCAccessExecutionRole"
        ]
      }
    }
  }
}
```

In this template, we created a `Resources` section, as we did in the first example. We created a resource with the `AWS::IAM::Role` type. In the `Properties` section, we created `AssumeRolePolicyDocument`. In this document, we indicated that the Lambda service can assume this policy on behalf of the Lambda function. In the `ManagedPolicyArns` section, we added a built-in IAM policy named `AWSLambdaVPCAccessExecutionRole`. This built-in policy has some permissions for executing in a VPC environment and logging to CloudWatch. Since almost every Lambda function needs these permissions by default, it is a good idea to assign it to our IAM role.

So far, it might seem that there are many new concepts, but this part was pretty boilerplate. You can check out the Lambda and IAM documentation to better understand what we do in this role, but you will surely never touch this resource again.

As a second step, we can create a custom IAM policy and attach it to the IAM role we just created. In this policy, we will define which AWS resources our role can access. As an example, we are going to add only the `s3:ListBuckets` permission, which will allow the Lambda function to list buckets in S3. Let's add this snippet as a new resource:

```
"LambdaCustomPolicy": {
  "Type": "AWS::IAM::Policy",
    "Properties": {
      "PolicyName": "LambdaCustomPolicy",
      "PolicyDocument": {
        "Version": "2012-10-17",
        "Statement": [
          {
            "Effect": "Allow",
            "Action": [
              "s3:ListBuckets"
            ],
            "Resource": "*"
          }
        ]
      },
      "Roles": [
        {
          "Ref": "LambdaExecutionRole"
        }
      ]
    }
}
```

Here, you can see a policy document written in the policy document syntax. You can learn about the policy document format in the AWS documentation. Take note of the Roles section of the resource. Here, we are attaching the IAM role we just created in the previous section of the template. `{"Ref": "RESOURCE_NAME"}` is an intrinsic function provided by the CloudFormation engine.

 CloudFormation provides a couple of intrinsic functions that you can use to refer to other resources, build up strings using variables and outputs from other resources and so on. You can get detailed information about those functions at `http://docs.aws.amazon.com/AWSCloudFormation/la test/UserGuide/intrinsic-function-reference.html`.

If we look at the properties section, the `AWS::IAM::Policy` resource type in the CloudFormation documentation, we will see that Roles is a property that accepts an array of IAM Role ARN. If we check the `Outputs` section of the `AWS::IAM::Role` resource type in the same documentation, we can see that the `Ref` intrinsic function gives the ARN of the policy as the output. This means that we can populate the Roles array with Ref function outputs. Here, we see the application of a very powerful feature of CloudFormation: referring to other resources. When we deploy this template, CloudFormation will automatically calculate the dependency graph between different resources, and in this case, it will first create the `LambdaCustomPolicy` resource before `LambdaExecutionRole` because the latter depends on the latter.

Before we move on to creating the Lambda function in the template, it is a good idea to write the Gradle script to deploy the CloudFormation template, so we can see that our template is working so far.

For the CloudFormation deployment, we will be using the Classmethod Inc.'s same Gradle plugin. We can start by adding the next snippet to the `build.gradle` file:

```
apply plugin: "jp.classmethod.aws.cloudformation"

cloudFormation {
    capabilityIam true
    templateFile project.file('cloudformation.template')
    templateBucket deploymentBucketName
    templateKeyPrefix "cfn-templates"
    stackName "serverlessbook"
}

awsCfnMigrateStack.dependsOn awsCfnUploadTemplate
```

The first line applies the plugin to the project. This plugin adds some tasks to our Gradle script, such as `awsCfnMigrateStackAndWaitCompleted`, `awsCfnMigrateStack`, and `awsCfnUploadTemplate`. The first one creates or updates the CloudFormation stack and waits until the provision is completed. The second one is very similar, but it does not wait until the template provision is completed. The latest one is also an important task; it uploads the CloudFormation template to the S3 bucket we created for deployment purposes. This is a requirement for the correct use of the plugin.

In the second section, we configure the CloudFormation stack. Let's take a look at these options:

- `capabilityIam`: Here, we let CloudFormation create IAM resources. Since we are creating IAM Roles and Policies, it is a must for us. With this flag disabled, the provision of our template will fail.
- `templateFile`: The location of the template file, which is the root directory in our case.
- `templateBucket`: The bucket name to upload the template. We basically pick the `deploymentBucketName` variable that we set previously.
- `templateKeyPrefix`: The prefix for the S3 bucket. You can pick anything.
- `stackName`: The CloudFormation stack name. Here, we pick here `serverlessbook`, or you can use the project's name.

After the CloudFormation configuration, we also indicate that the `awsCfnMigrateStack` task should run after the `awsCfnUploadTemplate` task.

After this configuration, we should create a new task to build and upload the artifacts and deploy the CloudFormation template. Now let's add this snippet to the end of our `build.gradle` file:

```
task deploy {
    configure(subprojects.findAll { it.name.startsWith("lambda-") }) {
        dependsOn it.uploadArtifactsToS3
    }
    finalizedBy awsCfnMigrateStackAndWaitCompleted
}
```

In this snippet, we create a deploy task. As you remember from the previous section, for any subproject whose name starts with `lambda-`, we created a task that is called `uploadArtifactsToS3`. Obviously, at the deployment stage, we should build all subprojects and upload them to S3. To accomplish this task, we iterate over all the subprojects that start with `lambda-` and add their `uploadArtifactsToS3` tasks as a dependency to deploy the task. And in the last line, we set the `awsCfnMigrateStackAndWaitCompleted` task as a final stage of the deploy.

It is time to try our deployment. Now execute the following command:

```
$ ./gradlew deploy
```

With those Gradles tasks, now you did not need to build a long CLI command to deploy your CloudFormation template and you can properly install the template and update whenever there is a change using parameters. As you can follow on the screen, the deploy task built and uploaded all the lambda subprojects-in our case, only lambda-test-and finally, it provisioned the CloudFormation template on our AWS account. We can now navigate to AWS Console and see our stack in the CloudFormation console. In the same way, we can launch the IAM console and see that an IAM Role is created with our stack name and a random string.

As a last step, we are going to modify our CloudFormation template with a Lambda function. Now let's open again the CloudFormation template file and add a new resource:

```
"RootGetLambda": {
    "Type": "AWS::Lambda::Function",
    "Properties": {
      "Handler": "com.serverlessbook.lambda.test.Handler",
      "Runtime": "java8",
      "Timeout": "300",
      "MemorySize": "1024",
      "Description": "Test lambda",
      "Role": {
        "Fn::GetAtt": [
          "LambdaExecutionRole",
          "Arn"
        ]
      },
      "Code": {
        "S3Bucket": "serverlessbook-us-east-1",
        "S3Key": "artifacts/lambda-test/1.0/12313123123.jar"
      }
    }
}
```

Now let's explain the configuration values step by step:

- `Handler`: Here, we set the handler method of our Lambda. You should remember this from the first chapter. We set any handler method that inherits from the `com.serverlessbook.lambda.LambdaHandler<I, O>` abstract class we implemented earlier.
- `Runtime`: This is the runtime engine. As we are using Java to author Lambda functions, we should put java8. Alternatives would be node4.3 or python2.7.
- `Timeout`: The timeout of the Lambda function in seconds. The default is 3 seconds and the maximum value can be 300 seconds.
- `MemorySize`: The allocated maximum memory value for the Lambda function. You can pick any value from 128 MB to 1536 MB, and the value must be a multiple of 64 MB. Note that with more memory, you also get more CPU, but the price per second also gets higher. For JVM, lower memory values are not recommended, and picking an insufficient memory size can cause unexpected crashes.

 For starting, you may choose 1024 MB and once you are sure that your application is working properly, you can reduce the memory size to find the sweet spot where you can get maximum reliability, performance and effective price.

- `Description`: A description for the Lambda function.
- `Role`: The IAM Role to be used to execute the Lambda function. Note that here, we are using another intrinsic function of CloudFormation. `"Fn::GetAtt":` `["LambdaExecutionRole", "Arn"]` gets the ARN of the IAM Role we created previously in our template.
- `Code`: Here, we specify the location of our JAR file in the S3 bucket.

You might have noted a big problem in this resource definition: in the `Code` section, firstly, we hardcode `S3Bucket` and secondly, in the `S3Key` option, we refer to a filename that does not exist. If we deploy this template, it will definitely fail because of these errors. We should inject the deployment bucket, project version, and deployment time variables into the template in order to dynamically construct the filename. At this step, we will introduce another powerful feature of CloudFormation: parameters. In our CloudFormation template, we can parameterize some values and use them in our resources. Whenever a value of a parameter changes, CloudFormation triggers an update for the relevant resources.

Now let's add the Parameters section to our template. Add the following snippet as a root element just before the `Resources` section:

```
"Parameters": {
    "DeploymentBucket": {
      "Type": "String",
      "Description": "S3 bucket name where built artifacts are deployed"
    },
    "ProjectVersion": {
      "Type": "String",
      "Description": "Project Version"
    },
    "DeploymentTime": {
      "Type": "String",
      "Description": "It is a timestamp value which shows the
         deployment time. Used to rotate sources."
    }
  }
```

Here, we define three mandatory parameters for our template. These parameters are very simple and have already been explained in their descriptions.

Now we have to use these parameters in our template to construct the filename for every deployment. As you may have noted in the section where we uploaded the artifacts, for every deployment, we are uploading a new JAR file with a timestamp. So, the location of the artifact can be shown as follows:

```
s3://DEPLOYMENT_BUCKET/artifacts/PROJECT_VERSION/DEPLOYMENT_TIME.jar
```

Then, we can modify the `Code` section as follows:

```
"Code": {
  "S3Bucket": {
    "Ref": "DeploymentBucket"
  },
  "S3Key": {
    "Fn::Join": [
      "",
      [
        "artifacts/",
        "lambda-test",
        "/",
        {
          "Ref": "ProjectVersion"
        },
        "/",
        {
```

```
        "Ref": "DeploymentTime"
      },
      ".jar"
    ]
  ]
}
}
```

For `S3Bucket`, we use the `Ref` intrinsic function again, and we directly inject the value of the `DeploymentBucket` parameter. For the `S3Key` value, we use the `Fn::Join` intrinsic function to construct the filename in the S3 bucket for every deployment. In this template, given that `ProjectVersion` is 1.0 and `DeploymentTime` is 1231231231312, the resulting filename would be `"artifacts/lambda-test/1.0/1231231231312.jar"`, which is really the filename of the JAR file that our Gradle builds and uploads to the S3 bucket.

Obviously, we have to modify our `build.gradle` file to inject these parameters to the CloudFormation template. Now add the following code to the end of the `cloudformation` {} block, just after `stackName`:

```
conventionMapping.stackParams = {
  return [
    DeploymentBucket: deploymentBucketName,
    ProjectVersion   : project.version,
    DeploymentTime   : deploymentTime
  ]
}
```

This snippet picks the variables from the script and injects them into the CloudFormation template. As these variables change for every deployment, the stack will get an update, and thus the latest code will always be live for our AWS Lambda function.

To give a try to our deployment, let's execute again:

```
$ ./gradlew deploy
```

When the deployment finishes, we can navigate to the AWS Console to see the newly created Lambda function. We can also see it with AWS CLI using the following command:

```
$ aws cloudformation describe-stack-resources
  --stack-name serverlessbook --region us-east-1
```

The output of this command will be similar to the following:

```
{
  "StackResources": [
    {
      "StackId": "arn:aws:cloudformation:us-east-1:423915886527:stack/
```

```
              serverlessbook/b0bbeaa0-9526-11e6-a1a8-5044763dbb7b",
          "ResourceStatus": "UPDATE_COMPLETE",
          "ResourceType": "AWS::IAM::Policy",
          "Timestamp": "2016-10-18T11:53:03.459Z",
          "StackName": "serverlessbook",
          "PhysicalResourceId": "serve-Lamb-1APLY9NQ6SAE1",
          "LogicalResourceId": "LambdaCustomPolicy"
      },
      {
          "StackId": "arn:aws:cloudformation:us-east-1:423915886527:stack/
              serverlessbook/b0bbeaa0-9526-11e6-a1a8-5044763dbb7b",
          "ResourceStatus": "UPDATE_COMPLETE",
          "ResourceType": "AWS::IAM::Role",
          "Timestamp": "2016-10-18T11:34:15.900Z",
          "StackName": "serverlessbook",
          "PhysicalResourceId": "serverlessbook-LambdaExecutionRole-
WOMSZF9W1R8D",
          "LogicalResourceId": "LambdaExecutionRole"
      },
      {
          "StackId": "arn:aws:cloudformation:us-east-1:423915886527:stack/
              serverlessbook/b0bbeaa0-9526-11e6-a1a8-5044763dbb7b",
          "ResourceStatus": "CREATE_COMPLETE",
          "ResourceType": "AWS::Lambda::Function",
          "Timestamp": "2016-10-18T14:47:24.281Z",
          "StackName": "serverlessbook",
          "PhysicalResourceId": "serverlessbook-TestLambda-1LCZZ94I7MQIY",
          "LogicalResourceId": "TestLambda"
      }
    ]
  }
```

As you can see, the Lambda function that is created by CloudFormation will have a random name, in this case, `serverlessbook-TestLambda-1LCZZ94I7MQIY`.

As we know the name of the function, we can now invoke it like we did in the first chapter:

```
$ aws lambda invoke --invocation-type RequestResponse \
                --region us-east-1 \
                --function-name
                  serverlessbook-TestLambda-1LCZZ94I7MQIY \
                --payload '{"value":"test"}' \
                --log-type Tail \
                /tmp/test.txt
```

Note that the function name shall be different in your configuration. If everything goes well, in the /tmp/test.txt file, you will see {"value":"test"} as the output of the Lambda function.

Summary

In this chapter, we looked at how to automate the deployment process using Gradle and CloudFormation. We modified our Gradle script to build all the artifacts automatically and deploy them to the S3 bucket, and finally, we created a Lambda function using CloudFormation.

In the next chapter, we will modify our Lambda function to respond to HTTP requests. We will introduce API Gateway and further develop our CloudFormation template to leverage the versioning feature of Lambda and API Gateway for the rollback ability we will bring in the future.

3
Hello Internet

In previous chapters, we looked at how to build standalone, event-based Lambda functions. Lambda functions were code pieces living in the cloud that respond to different events, such as a new file in S3 bucket or an SNS notification, such as what we will see in following chapters. However, at this stage, maybe our simplest requirements would be to invoke the lambda function with an HTTP request, thus having a fully serverless REST API.

Thanks to API Gateway, it is possible to create a REST API that responds to HTTP requests. API Gateway replaces servlets, servlet containers, application servers, and basically the HTTP layer. When a request arrives at API Gateway, it decides where to route this request, transforms the input, invokes the "backend", and sends back the response to the client.

API Gateway can proxy to many types of backends, and it can be configured separately by the REST resource and the HTTP method. It can proxy requests to a custom HTTP API, to an AWS API, or-most importantly-to a Lambda function. For example, you might have an on-premise REST API and you can route the users resource of your API to that application, while you can route other requests to lambda functions. You can even proxy to AWS APIs, so you can allow users to upload their pictures to an S3 bucket after authorizing them via another Lambda function. This is one of the examples we will see in this book and you will learn how easy it is to build an image upload service using AWS offerings.

In this chapter, we will introduce API Gateway and connect some Lambda functions to HTTP resources and methods. This chapter is extremely important because we will introduce complicated CloudFormation structures and a lot of new concepts. Additionally, we will cover CloudFront, the CDN solution of AWS. With CloudFront, we will enable some HTTP features such as HTTP/2 or IPv6, which are currently not available for API Gateway out of box.

As for this chapter, we will just cover how to create a REST API using the very simple test function we developed in previous chapters. Throughout the book, we will develop more Lambda functions and REST endpoints. These will extend our API Gateway configuration, but it is important that you understand the basics for now. Also, you will explore how to configure a CDN that can be useful even for classical approaches. At the end of the chapter, we will introduce our second Lambda function, which will authorize API calls.

We will cover the following topics in this chapter:

- Setting up API Gateway
- Creating a REST endpoint using our current Lambda function
- Manipulating an HTTP request data and the incoming Lambda response
- Setting up CloudFront CDN for enhanced HTTP properties
- Decoupling a Lambda function to authenticate API calls with a Bearer token

Setting up API Gateway

In this section, we will start with extending our CloudFormation template.

First of all, we should start with some boilerplate. In the previous chapter, we had mentioned **CloudWatch Logs**, the service that AWS provides to store logs in a central place. API Gateway also uses CloudWatch to store HTTP logs and, like all services that try to access to other services, needs an **IAM role**. In this IAM role, we should give access to the apigateway.amazonaws.com service to access the CloudWatch logs and deliver this role to API Gateway as the `AWS::ApiGateway::Account` resource. Now let's open our CloudFormation template and just prepend these lines to the `Resources` section:

```
"ApiGatewayCloudwatchRole": {
    "Type": "AWS::IAM::Role",
    "Properties": {
      "AssumeRolePolicyDocument": {
        "Version": "2012-10-17",
        "Statement": [
          {
            "Effect": "Allow",
            "Principal": {
              "Service": [
                "apigateway.amazonaws.com"
              ]
            },
            "Action": "sts:AssumeRole"
          }
```

```
      ]
    },
    "Path": "/",
    "ManagedPolicyArns": [
      "arn:aws:iam::aws:policy/service-
role/AmazonAPIGatewayPushToCloudWatchLogs"
    ]
  }
},
"ApiGatewayAccount": {
  "Type": "AWS::ApiGateway::Account",
  "Properties": {
    "CloudWatchRoleArn": {
      "Fn::GetAtt": [
        "ApiGatewayCloudwatchRole",
        "Arn"
      ]
    }
  }
}
}
```

Considering you may be familiar with the syntax, you should understand what are we doing here. Basically, we are creating a role with the `arn:aws:iam::aws:policy/service-role/AmazonAPIGatewayPushToCloudWatchLogs` built-in IAM policy, which allows you to write to the CloudWatch role. In the `AssumeRolePolicyDocument` section, we indicate that `apigateway.amazonaws.com`, the IAM entity API Gateway uses internally, can assume the role, so it can write to the logs. If you deploy the project at this stage and open the **Settings** tab of API Gateway Console on AWS Console, you shall see the newly created IAM role in the **CloudWatch log role ARN** box. This is a one-time step that should be done once per account per region.

Creating the API

Following the REST principles, API Gateway consists of different parts: REST API, stage, resources, and methods. If we analyze an API Gateway URL, it is easier to understand `https://51xda3cqkj.execute-api.us-east-1.amazonaws.com/production/ping`.

Here, `51xda3cqkj` is the API ID, while `production` is the stage and `ping` is a resource. When you set up an API Gateway, you first create a REST API, so reserve an API ID that will build the URL of the API in future. Then, you create resources with static routes such as `/ping` or with parameters such as `/users/{id}` and finally, you create HTTP methods under these resources.

API Gateway offers a couple of options as the backend to HTTP methods. For instance, you can proxy native AWS APIs with limited permissions, so, for example, your users can upload files to S3 on your behalf. You can use API Gateway as a proxy to an existing custom REST API you built with another platform, and finally, and most importantly for us, you can invoke Lambda functions to process a request and return a response. For all the options, API Gateway provides a set of request and response transformation possibilities. For example, as we already know, Lambda functions accept some JSON strings as input and return JSON responses. They do not know, and mostly are not interested in, who is invoking them; they just process the input and return an output. At this stage, the transformation capabilities of API Gateway become very important. Using API Gateway, we will map HTTP request parameters to JSON properties and create a JSON object to send to the Lambda function. Also, we can map back the returning object to HTTP response parameters such as response headers or the response body. API Gateway uses **Apache Velocity Template Language (VTL)** for this mapping process, and in the following sections, we will be writing some transformations with this language.

To start with creating our API Gateway stack, we can add a `AWS::ApiGateway::RestApi` resource type just below the `AWS::ApiGateway::Account` we just created. `AWS::ApiGateway::RestApi` is a simple resource with minimum properties:

```
"RestApi": {
  "Type": "AWS::ApiGateway::RestApi",
  "Properties": {
    "Name": {
      "Ref": "AWS::StackName"
    }
  }
}
```

For the sake of simplicity, we named the API using the `AWS::StackName` variable, which means that if you are following our naming convention, this will be `serverlessbook`.

If you want, you can deploy now; open the API Gateway console and check whether your new API is created.

Creating the resource

After we create the API, we can now create our first resource, which will be a test resource, and remove it later. We can add these lines to the end of our resources in order to create the resource:

```
"TestResource": {
    "Type": "AWS::ApiGateway::Resource",
```

```
"Properties": {
  "PathPart": "test",
  "RestApiId": {
    "Ref": "RestApi"
  },
  "ParentId": {
    "Fn::GetAtt": [
      "RestApi",
      "RootResourceId"
    ]
  }
}
}
```

If we analyze this resource, we can see that the resource type is
AWS::ApiGateway::Resource . In the properties part, we can see PathPart , and we set it as test. It will create a REST resource and will be invoked when https://base_url/test is requested. Here, we can use brackets to create a dynamic parameter. For example, {test} would match both https://base_url/1 and https://base_url/2, and we can use these parameters to pass to our Lambda function. The RestApiId property refers to the AWS::ApiGateway::RestApi resource we just created, and ParentId refers to the RootResourceId value of the RestApi resource.

> This is a bit tricky. Normally, you create resources referring to their parent resources. For example, to create a resource such as /users/{id}/picture, you have to create the users, {id}, and picture resources separately, and for each resource, you have to refer to the previous one. But for the users resource, you do not have a parent resource. In that case, you should refer to the RootResourceId value of the REST API.

Creating the method

After we create the resource, we can create the very first HTTP method under that. This part is maybe the trickiest one because it needs many configurations and we are going to introduce new concepts. First, let's add the method configuration and then let's discuss it line by line:

```
"TestGetMethod": {
  "Type": "AWS::ApiGateway::Method",
  "Properties": {
    "HttpMethod": "GET",
    "RestApiId": {
```

```
      "Ref": "RestApi"
    },
    "ResourceId": {
      "Ref": "TestResource"
    },
    "AuthorizationType": "NONE",
    "RequestParameters": {
      "method.request.querystring.value": "True"
    },
    "MethodResponses": [
      {
        "StatusCode": "200"
      }
    ],
    "Integration": {
      "Type": "AWS",
      "Uri": {
        "Fn::Sub": "arn:aws:apigateway:${AWS::Region}:lambda:path/
          2015-03-31/functions/${TestLambda.Arn}/invocations"
      },
      "IntegrationHttpMethod": "POST",
      "RequestParameters": {
        "integration.request.querystring.value":
          "method.request.querystring.value"
      },
      "RequestTemplates": {
        "application/json": "{\"value\":\"$input.params('value')\"}"
      },
      "PassthroughBehavior": "NEVER",
      "IntegrationResponses": [
        {
          "SelectionPattern": ".*",
          "StatusCode": "200"
        }
      ]
    }
  }
}
}
```

Here, we define a GET method with our test Lambda function as the backend. The
HttpMethod, RestApi, and ResourceId properties are very simple. We define the GET
HTTP method under the REST API and /test resource we have just created.

We set the `AuthorizationType` property to `NONE` to allow this endpoint to have public access. In the following chapter, we will look at how we can integrate a second Lambda function just to authorize API Gateway endpoints.

In `RequestParameters`, we define which request parameters are to be caught from the request in order to pass them to the Lambda backend. Here, we get the `value` query parameter, setting `method.request.querystring.value` to `True` and the `Accept` header, setting `method.request.header.Accept` to `True` . If we want to use any of the request parameters, we must define them strictly; if not, they will be ignored and not passed to the backend.

In the `MethodResponses` part, we define only 200, which will be the default status code of our method. If we want other status code-say, 201-we must declare them separately and map them to different outputs of the backend. We will explore this feature later.

So far, we have declared the HTTP interface, filtered some request parameters, and declared possible HTTP codes. Now in the `Integration` part, we show you how to pass these values to the Lambda function.

Some of the Integration part is boilerplate. The type should be set to AWS and the URI should be constructed properly. Normally, the URL should be like this:
```
arn:aws:apigateway:us-
east-1:lambda:path/2015-03-31/functions/arn:aws:lambda:us-
east-1:423915886527:function:serverlessbook-
TestLambda-6G0CT84ER5SI/invocations.
```

Here, there are only two variables: the first is the region and the second one is Lambda's ARN, which is between functions and invocations word. Then, we can write this using this expression:
```
arn:aws:apigateway:${AWS::Region}:lambda:path/2015-03-31/functions/${Te
stLambda.Arn}/invocations
```

API Gateway sends a POST request to this URL, so `IntegrationHttpMethod` should be POST.

`RequestParameters` maps the values we fetch from the request to the backend side. Here, we map the value query string and the Accept header to the integration request.

In the `RequestTemplates` section, we finally create the event to be sent to the Lambda function. Here, we can use the Apache Velocity language. In our example, we create a JSON using the `$input.params()` built-in function. For now, we keep the event simple, but in the AWS documentation, you can see more options, and in the following chapters, we will be using more options to build our JSON. At this stage, we can use a lot of variables such as User Agent or client IP using this section and inject them to the underlying Lambda function. This is a good opportunity to isolate the complexity of the HTTP request from the Lambda function. In this way, the Lambda function does not have to deal with extracting request information but can just consume the provided values. Also, note that we used `application/json` as the key of the JSON. This means that only when the Accept header is `application/json` will this integration not work. The next option, `PassthroughBehavior`, specifies how the method request body of an unmapped content type will be passed through the integration request to the backend without transformation. As we set it to `NEVER` and we only have the mapping for `application/json`, if the request comes with a content type other than `application/json`, API Gateway will respond with **415 Unsupported Media Type**. Here, we force the client to use the Content-Type header and we comply with the REST standards.

Finally, in the `IntegrationResponses` section, we map different responses to different status code. Basically, we match all responses to the 200 status code here. Alternatively, we could map all the responses that include the `ERROR` string to the 500 status code. Note that here, we pass through the response we get from Lambda to the client. We could also apply a transformation to modify the response we get before we send it to the client.

 It is very basic implementation of the API Gateway and it does not leverage some features. In the following chapters, we will have more complicated integrations and it is recommended that you take a look at the AWS documentation in order to see which options are available.

Now you can deploy the stack and open the API Gateway console to see the options set for us. Go to the `GET` method we created and try to execute it using the **Test** button. As we defined them as the input, the test screen will have two fields to enter the value query string and the Accept header. Write some test values to them and press the **Test** button.

Yes, it failed! It complains about insufficient permissions.

Configuring Lambda permissions

As we stated at the beginning of this chapter, every AWS resource is an entity and some services and our own accounts are actors. In this case, we have an entity, Lambda function, and an actor, API Gateway, which tries to invoke the Lambda function . On the other hand, we did not allow API Gateway to access our Lambda function; therefore, it cannot invoke it.

To solve this issue, we have to add an extra resource to our CloudFormation file, which is AWS::Lambda::Permission . Here is our snippet to be added to the end of the Resources section:

```
    "TestLambdaPermission": {
      "Type": "AWS::Lambda::Permission",
      "Properties": {
        "Action": "lambda:InvokeFunction",
        "FunctionName": {
          "Ref": "TestLambda"
        },
        "Principal": "apigateway.amazonaws.com",
        "SourceArn": {
          "Fn::Sub": "arn:aws:execute-
api:${AWS::Region}:${AWS::AccountId}:${RestApi}/*"
        }
      }
    }
```

Here, we give lambda:InvokeFunction permission to the apigateway.amazonaws.com entity when the Source ARN matches the API we are creating in this stack.

After redeploying the stack, you can test the method again using the **Test** button, and you can see the result.

 You might think that this process is a bit complicated. Most of these issues, including permission problems, are solved when you create the API using AWS Console. However, as we decided to create our infrastructure completely with code, we must take care of some steps manually.

Deploying the API

So far, we've defined the API and its resource, but these changes are not in production until we create a deployment. To enable the API in production, we should deploy it.

If you have read the CloudFormation documentation, you might have seen the `AWS::ApiGateway::Deployment` resource. It creates an API Gateway deployment perfectly. However, it has a caveat; it creates an immutable resource, so in order to redeploy the latest changes whenever you update the CloudFormation stack, you must add a new Deployment resource. We do not know why such a bad design decision has been taken, but obviously, this resource does not meet our automation needs.

To overcome this issue, we will leverage a very nice feature of CloudFormation: Lambda backed custom resources. We will use a small Lambda function that will be triggered whenever the CloudFormation stack is updated and will invoke the AWS API to create a deployment. Specially for this book, the necessary Node.js code is created for every region and uploaded to S3 buckets, and we will be using it directly in our template.

 If you want to check the content of the code, you can download it from https://s3.amazonaws.com/serverless-arch-us-east-1/serverless.zip.

We can first create the necessary role and the Lambda function, and then we can place it at the beginning of the `Resources` section:

```
"DeploymentLambdaRole": {
  "Type": "AWS::IAM::Role",
  "Properties": {
    "AssumeRolePolicyDocument": {
      "Version": "2012-10-17",
      "Statement": [
        {
          "Effect": "Allow",
          "Principal": {
            "Service": [
              "lambda.amazonaws.com"
            ]
          },
          "Action": [
            "sts:AssumeRole"
          ]
        }
      ]
    },
    "Path": "/",
    "ManagedPolicyArns": [
      "arn:aws:iam::aws:policy/service-
role/AWSLambdaVPCAccessExecutionRole"
    ],
    "Policies": [
```

```json
        {
          "PolicyName": "LambdaExecutionPolicy",
          "PolicyDocument": {
            "Version": "2012-10-17",
            "Statement": [
              {
                "Effect": "Allow",
                "Action": [
                  "lambda:PublishVersion",
                  "apigateway:POST"
                ],
                "Resource": [
                  "*"
                ]
              }
            ]
          }
        }
      ]
    }
  },
  "DeploymentLambda": {
    "Type": "AWS::Lambda::Function",
    "Properties": {
      "Role": {
        "Fn::GetAtt": [
          "PublishNewVersionRole",
          "Arn"
        ]
      },
      "Handler": "index.handler",
      "Runtime": "nodejs4.3",
      "Code": {
        "S3Bucket": {
          "Fn::Sub": "serverless-arch-${AWS::Region}"
        },
        "S3Key": "serverless.zip"
      }
    }
  }
```

We will skip explaining this part step by step, but as you can understand with your current AWS experience, here, we create an IAM role that grants `apigateway:POST` and `lambda:PublishVersion` permissions. You might ask at this point why we also granted the `lambda:PublishVersion` permission, which we have never seen so far. That is because in the following stages, we will also version our Lambda functions for the rollback capability, and this Lambda function will also help us for that. To not repeat the same process, we just prepare the IAM role for this feature.

After we create the necessary Lambda function, we can add the custom resource to the tail of the `Resources` section:

```
"ApiDeployment": {
    "DependsOn": [
      "TestGetMethod"
    ],
    "Type": "Custom::ApiDeployment",
    "Properties": {
      "ServiceToken": {
        "Fn::GetAtt": [
          "DeploymentLambda",
          "Arn"
        ]
      },
      "RestApiId": {
        "Ref": "RestApi"
      },
      "StageName": "production",
      "DeploymentTime": {
        "Ref": "DeploymentTime"
      }
    }
  }
}
```

This is the standard syntax for Lambda-backed custom resources. Only `ServiceToken` is mandatory, and it should be the ARN of the Lambda function. Other parameters are passed to the Lambda function in the event and our Lambda function consumes them to create a new API deployment via API calls and returns the result. A Lambda-backed custom resource is an advanced topic of CloudFormation. Here, we do not dive deep into the details since it is directly related to our topic, but if you are more interested in the topic, it is recommended that you read the AWS documentation: (http://docs.aws.amazon.com/AWSCloudFormation/latest/UserGuide/template -custom-resources-lambda.html).

If your application grows and you hit the limits of CloudFormation, you can write other custom resources and keep your infrastructure in CloudFormation.

After this step, we can deploy the project again, and this time, our API should be publicly available. To see the URL of your API, you can navigate to the AWS Console. If you want to see it via CLI, you can run the following command:

```
$ aws cloudformation describe-stack-resources --region us-east-1
  --stack-name serverlessbook
```

This will print the created resources for our stack. Among them, you can see the `AWS::ApiGateway::RestApi` resource, such as the following JSON:

```
{
  "StackId": "arn:aws:cloudformation:us-east-
1:423915886527:stack/serverlessbook/8bb69620-9dd6-11e6-9003-50d5cd24fac6",
  "ResourceStatus": "CREATE_COMPLETE",
  "ResourceType": "AWS::ApiGateway::RestApi",
  "Timestamp": "2016-11-13T15:06:14.375Z",
  "StackName": "serverlessbook",
  "PhysicalResourceId": "eciv8og4wj",
  "LogicalResourceId": "RestApi"
}
```

Here, `PhysicalResourceId` is our API's ID and the resulting URL would then be `https://eciv8og4wj.execute-api.us-east-1.amazonaws.com/production`.

Let's try to access our first endpoint using CURL in the verbose mode:

```
$ curl -v https://eciv8og4wj.execute-api.us-east-1.amazonaws.com/
production/test?value=hello+world
*   Hostname was NOT found in DNS cache
*     Trying 52.222.157.193...
*   Connected to eciv8og4wj.execute-api.us-east-1.amazonaws.com
(52.222.157.193) port 443 (#0)
*   successfully set certificate verify locations:
*     CAfile: none
      CApath: /etc/ssl/certs
*   SSLv3, TLS handshake, Client hello (1):
*   SSLv3, TLS handshake, Server hello (2):
*   SSLv3, TLS handshake, CERT (11):
*   SSLv3, TLS handshake, Server key exchange (12):
*   SSLv3, TLS handshake, Server finished (14):
*   SSLv3, TLS handshake, Client key exchange (16):
*   SSLv3, TLS change cipher, Client hello (1):
*   SSLv3, TLS handshake, Finished (20):
*   SSLv3, TLS change cipher, Client hello (1):
```

```
* SSLv3, TLS handshake, Finished (20):
* SSL connection using ECDHE-RSA-AES128-GCM-SHA256
* Server certificate:
*       subject: C=US; ST=Washington; L=Seattle; O=Amazon.com, Inc.;
CN=*.execute-api.us-east-1.amazonaws.com
*       start date: 2016-06-08 00:00:00 GMT
*       expire date: 2017-07-08 23:59:59 GMT
*       subjectAltName: eciv8og4wj.execute-api.us-east-1.amazonaws.com
matched
*       issuer: C=US; O=Symantec Corporation; OU=Symantec Trust Network;
CN=Symantec Class 3 Secure Server CA - G4
*       SSL certificate verify ok.
> GET /production/test?value=hello+world HTTP/1.1
> User-Agent: curl/7.35.0
> Host: eciv8og4wj.execute-api.us-east-1.amazonaws.com
> Accept: */*
>
< HTTP/1.1 200 OK
< Content-Type: application/json
< Content-Length: 23
< Connection: keep-alive
< Date: Mon, 21 Nov 2016 21:16:15 GMT
< x-amzn-RequestId: bc4e5395-b02f-11e6-91ae-fd48641b4f02
< X-Amzn-Trace-Id: Root=1-5833641f-d12570a2d1e70be03bd61c8f
< X-Cache: Miss from cloudfront
< Via: 1.1 ec27b2a550cb7db6ef54f74603010b29.cloudfront.net (CloudFront)
< X-Amz-Cf-Id: qN1K2jmEyeBMPSrPIUejXyTVwj8BhxZTNm4CCiYaITnTw52WDTlewg==
<
* Connection #0 to host eciv8og4wj.execute-api.us-east-1.amazonaws.com
left intact
{"value":"hello world"}
```

Great! Our first serverless REST API is online and working.

Setting up the CloudFront CDN distribution

As you may have noted, so far, we only have a URL generated by AWS. It is not friendly nor does it use our custom SSL certificate, so we may want to replace it with a custom domain and an SSL certificate. The API Gateway supports it out of the box, but it is very poor support, and first, it needs the certificate to be copies and pasted manually, which is not the best way of enabling SSL, especially for big corporates.

AWS is offering a better solution to solve all these issues and cover the lack of some features of API Gateway. CloudFront is the CDN offering of AWS, and it supports many features. Here, we will set up a CloudFront distribution, which will proxy API Gateway and we will gain many features, such as the following:

- Free SSL support via **ACM (Amazon Certificate Manager)**
- HTTP/2 and IPv6 support
- GZIP compression
- HTTP caching

 For users who are geographically away from the region our API is deployed on, API Gateway will suffer from higher network latencies. On the other hand, CloudFront has many edge locations all around the world, which have very good connection quality between each other. When we put a CloudFront distribution between the API Gateway and the user, the user will connect to the nearest edge location and then enjoy the fast speed between the edge location and the deployment point. Therefore, it is always a good idea to leverage CloudFront for web applications.

CloudFront configuration is not too complicated. We can start with the following snippet and check out line by line what is going on:

```
"CloudformationDistribution": {
    "Type": "AWS::CloudFront::Distribution",
    "Properties": {
        "DistributionConfig": {
            "Enabled": "true",
            "HttpVersion": "http2",
            "Origins": [
                {
                    "DomainName": {
                      "Fn::Sub": "${RestApi}.execute-api.
                       ${AWS::Region}.amazonaws.com"
                    },
                    "OriginPath": "/production",
                    "Id": "APIGATEWAY",
                    "CustomOriginConfig": {
                        "OriginProtocolPolicy": "https-only"
                    }
                }
            ],
            "DefaultCacheBehavior": {
              "TargetOriginId": "APIGATEWAY",
              "Compress": true,
              "AllowedMethods": [
```

```
                    "DELETE",
                    "GET",
                    "HEAD",
                    "OPTIONS",
                    "PATCH",
                    "POST",
                    "PUT"
                ],
                "ForwardedValues": {
                    "QueryString": "true",
                    "Cookies": {
                        "Forward": "none"
                    },
                    "Headers": [
                        "Accept",
                        "Content-Type",
                        "Authorization"
                    ]
                },
                "DefaultTTL": 0,
                "MaxTTL": 0,
                "MinTTL": 0,
                "ViewerProtocolPolicy": "redirect-to-https"
            }
        }
    }
}
```

First, we define the resource as the `AWS::CloudFront::Distribution` type and then we get a couple of configuration options.

We start with setting `Enabled` to true which. `HttpVersion` is used to enable the recently brought HTTP/2 support. This support is free and there is no reason not to enable it since it is also backward-compatible with clients that do not support it. After that, we start defining an origin to be proxied, which is the API Gateway in our case. It is possible to define more than one origin and route among them using different paths.

For now, we have only one origin, but in the following chapters, we will define an S3 bucket as another origin to show profile pictures of our users. With `DomainName`, we construct the domain name of our API Gateway endpoint using the `Fn::Sub` function and variables from other resources. `OriginPath` is very useful in our case: we set it to /production in order to omit this unnecessary part of the URL. `Id` is a custom name for our origin. In `CustomOriginConfig`, we define using which protocol CloudFront will use to access the backend. API Gateway supports only HTTPS, so we pick the https-only option here. After defining the origin, we now define the default cache behavior. CloudFront can act differently for different paths. Say, if you have a directory that has only static files, you can create a different cache configuration for that path. If CloudFront cannot find any special cache configuration matching with that path, it uses the default cache behavior. In the `DefaultCacheBehavior` section, we first declare that all requests should be fulfilled using the `APIGATEWAY` origin. Compress is an option to enable the `GZIP` compression. It is a must to have this compression, and unfortunately, API Gateway does not provide it, so we can overcome this problem by enabling this option, so our clients will get compressed results. `AllowedMethods` declares which HTTP methods we are supporting. For a typical REST API, all the HTTP methods available make sense, so we enable all of them. `ForwardedValues` is a important option. Here, we define which HTTP request values we want to forward to the backend. For now, we do not enable caching on the CloudFront side, and we will do that later when we build some real endpoints and decide that it is appropriate to cache results. However, at this stage, we should know that CloudFront creates the cache key using the forwarded values. For this configuration, we forward all the query strings and forward none of the cookies because for a REST API, cookies do not make any sense. We only forward the `Accept`, `Content-Type`, and `Authorization` headers. If we had enabled caching, for each client with a different `Accept`, `Content-Type`, and `Authorization` header, the cached response would be different. If you want more fine-grained configuration, for every endpoint, you can create a new cache behavior configuration and define exactly which query parameters and headers to pass to the backend. At this stage, for the sake of simplicity, we leave this as a generic configuration.

CloudFront configuration is almost complete with a default CloudFront domain. At this stage, we can deploy the application and wait until the CloudFront configuration is deployed. This time, deployment will take more time than usual because CloudFront has a lot of machines all over the world and the propagation of a new configuration takes time. Gradle will probably time out, but no worries; the deployment of the CloudFormation stack will continue and you can observe it on the AWS console.

When deployment finishes, you can navigate to the CloudFront section of the AWS Console. There, you can see your new CDN distribution and read the domain name assigned automatically by CloudFront. You can try to send a request to the CloudFront distribution now:

```
$ curl https://d3foeb7gudycc2.cloudfront.net/test?
  value=hello+world {"value":"hello world"}
```

Note that the URL you have will be different than the preceding command.

We are not finished yet because we have still not enabled the custom domain.

Setting up the custom domain

For the custom domain support, we will use **Route 53** , the great built-in DNS solution of AWS. We assume that you already have one personal domain name registered. We will create a hosted zone in Route 53 for a subdomain of this domain. Your domain can be registered in any registrar; if you do not have any, you can also use Route 53 to register one.

First, let's start with creating a new parameter in our CloudFormation template:

```
"DomainName": {
  "Type": "String",
  "Description": "Domain Name to serve the application"
}
```

Now we should assign a value to this parameter in our `build.gradle`, editing the `stackParams` block as follows:

```
conventionMapping.stackParams = {
  return [
    DeploymentBucket: deploymentBucketName,
    ProjectVersion  : project.version,
    DeploymentTime  : deploymentTime,
    DomainName      : "serverlessbook.example.com"
  ]
}
```

Note that you should change the `DomainName` parameter as per your domain. Adding this snippet will create a hosted zone for your domain:

```
"Route53HostedZone": {
  "Type": "AWS::Route53::HostedZone",
  "Properties": {
    "HostedZoneConfig": {
      "Comment": "Serverless Book Project Hosted Zone"
    },
    "Name": {
      "Ref": "DomainName"
    }
  }
}
```

Now we should create a DNS record under the hosted zone we have just created. Again, with CloudFormation, we can add this snippet to the `Resources` section:

```
"DNSRecord": {
  "Type": "AWS::Route53::RecordSetGroup",
  "Properties": {
    "HostedZoneId": {
      "Ref": "Route53HostedZone"
    },
    "RecordSets": [
      {
        "Name": {
          "Ref": "DomainName"
        },
        "Type": "A",
        "AliasTarget": {
          "HostedZoneId": "Z2FDTNDATAQYW2",
          "DNSName": {
            "Fn::GetAtt": [
              "CloudformationDistribution",
              "DomainName"
            ]
          }
        }
      }
    ]
  }
}
```

This configuration is very simple until the `AliasTarget` section. Aliases are a powerful feature of Route 53. Instead of `CNAME` records, we can define `Alias` records that point directly to AWS resources, such as **ELBs (Elastic Load Balancer)**, CloudFormation distributions, and so on. This is a Route 53-specific record type and it does not have any equivalent in DNS standards. A big advantage of Alias records is that unlike CNAME records, they are free of charge. Also, if we had defined the CloudFront distribution as a CNAME record, clients would have to resolve one more step to reach the final IP address. With Alias records, we get rid of this overhead. `HostedZoneId` is also an **internal AWS thing** . It is documented by AWS and the only thing we publicly know is that we must give this information when we create an alias record to CloudFront distributions. This is boilerplate.

We can now deploy our application and let CloudFormation create the DNS records for us.

After the deployment, we can navigate to the Route 53 console to see the hosted zone created for us. Here, we should note the NS values for the hosted zone. Now you should create an NS record pointing to this subdomain in your parent domain and put NS values of the Route 53 hosted zone as values.

If you configured your DNS well, you can ping the domain and it should resolve one of the CloudFront IP addresses.

Creating an SSL certificate

Recently, AWS launched a service that issues free SSL certificates. **ACM (Amazon Certificate Manager)** is a revolutionary service that makes it easy to create SSL certificates and, additionally, it takes care of certificate rotation for you.

We will now create a new ACM certificate for our domain. This snippet will do that for us:

```
"SSLCertificate": {
  "Type": "AWS::CertificateManager::Certificate",
  "Properties": {
    "DomainName": {
      "Ref": "DomainName"
    },
    "DomainValidationOptions": [
      {
        "DomainName": {
          "Ref": "DomainName"
        },
        "ValidationDomain": "example.com"
      }
```

```
        ]
      }
   }
```

When you deploy the stack, you will receive an email to the administrator of your domain. Until you approve the certificate request using the link you find in this mail, CloudFormation deployment will not finish. So check the email registered with your domain. To see which email addresses AWS tries, go to the Amazon Certificate Manager section of the AWS Console and check out the certificate. You can get more information about this process at http://docs.aws.amazon.com/acm/latest/userguide/gs-acm-vali date.html.

As a last step, we should define our domain name as CNAME to our CloudFront distribution and provide the SSL certificate ID to enable the custom domain in CloudFront.

Now let's edit the DistributionConfig part of our CloudFront distribution, as follows:

```
"DistributionConfig": {
    "Aliases": [
        {
            "Ref": "DomainName"
        }
    ],
    "ViewerCertificate": {
        "SslSupportMethod": "sni-only",
        "AcmCertificateArn": {
            "Ref": "SSLCertificate"
        }
    },
    "Enabled": "true",
    . . .
```

Here, we define the DomainName variable as an alias, so CloudFront also responds to the request coming from this domain. In the ViewerCertificate part, we refer to the certificate we have just created and as SslSupportMethod , we define sni-only. Valid values for this option are vip and sni-only . If you specify vip, CloudFront uses dedicated IP addresses for your content and can respond to HTTPS requests from any viewer. However, you must request permission to use this feature, and you incur additional monthly charges. If you specify sni-only, CloudFront can only respond to HTTPS requests from viewers that support **Server Name Indication (SNI)**.

All modern browsers support SNI, but some browsers still in use don't support SNI. For most cases, SNI is just fine, so we pick this option. Please note that also some old versions of Java and some testing frameworks do not support SNI, so consider your use case.

Now we can deploy our application again, but wait a bit more because it is a CloudFront change that takes more time than usual.

We can try to access our API now, this time using our custom domain:

```
$ curl https://serverlessbook.example.com?value=hello+world
  {"value":"hello world"}
```

We can see that we have a fully serverless REST API, with custom domain and SSL support, working with HTTP/2 protocol!

Authenticating API calls

For our application, authenticating API calls has an important place. Since we have a forum application, it is very normal that while some endpoints are public (for example, forum topics), some of them are private and should be authenticated and the user should be authorized before they are called. For example, only the authorized user should be able to change their personal details or password or their profile picture.

So far, it might seem to be a very simple task to implement authentication. With the knowledge we have obtained in this chapter, we could extract credentials from the HTTP request and our Lambda handler could verify them against a data layer and decide to allow or not to allow the request. However, although it is technically possible, with this approach, there are some caveats, such as the following:

- Mixing authentication logic and business logic together. Violation of the Separation of Concerns principle.
- Losing the ability of authenticating API calls with a backend without Lambda.

The very first example of the second case is when you proxy AWS calls using API Gateway. We have already mentioned that we will be implementing an S3 API proxy to let users update their profile pictures. In this case, we will not have a Lambda backend because it is sufficient to manipulate the request and pass it through to the S3 API. On the other hand, we must be sure that an authenticated user is sending this profile picture change request and we need this user's ID to save to the S3 bucket.

At this point, API Gateway provides a very useful feature and lets us define custom authorizers for endpoints. Custom authorizers are called automatically by API Gateway just before the actual request is processed and they can allow or disallow the request. If the custom authorizer sends a block signal, the API Gateway automatically sends 4xx response code, indicating that the caller user is not allowed to call the endpoint. If the authorizer decides that the caller credentials are valid, it sends an approval signal to API Gateway along with a principal ID (for example, user ID, username, or any unique identifier for the caller entity) and this value is also passed through the backend. In this way, the Lambda function that includes the business logic does not have to deal with the authentication and authorization process.

Implementing basic authorization

In this section, we will implement a very basic custom authorizer, which will decide whether to allow or disallow requests in the function of a hardcoded authorization token. This authorizer will not have any data layer at this stage but will be a great start for some real business logic, because in the next chapter, we will start with an authentication server that is injected to this authorizer lambda via the dependency injection pattern, and in the following chapter, we will connect it to a DynamoDB database for production quality authentication.

First, let's start writing some Java code for our authorizer. Now we will create a new Lambda function in its own module called `lambda-authorizer`. We can create the directory structure by running this command on our project's home directory:

```
$ mkdir -p lambda-authorizer/src/main/java/com/
   serverlessbook/lambda/authorizer
```

To define `lambda-authorizer` as a submodule, we must add this folder to the `settings.gradle` file. We can accomplish this using this simple command:

```
$ echo "include 'lambda-authorizer'" >> settings.gradle
```

Before we go further, we should understand the input event API Gateway sends to an authorizer Lambda and the output it expects.

When API Gateway receives a request for a REST method that uses a custom authorizer, it populates the following payload and invokes the authorizer Lambda with it:

```
{
  "type":"TOKEN",
  "authorizationToken":"<caller-supplied-token>",
  "methodArn":"arn:aws:execute-api:<regionId>:<accountId>:
    <apiId>/<stage>/<method>/<resourcePath>"
}
```

Using this payload, the authorizer Lambda should decide whether to allow or disallow the method execution and return a response in the following format:

```
{
  "principalId": "xxxxxxxx", // The principal user identification
    associated with the token send by the client.
  "policyDocument": {
    "Version": "2012-10-17",
    "Statement": [
      {
        "Action": "execute-api:Invoke",
        "Effect": "Allow|Deny",
        "Resource": "arn:aws:execute-api:<regionId>:<accountId>:
          <appId>/<stage>/<httpVerb>/[<resource>/<httpVerb>/[...]]"
      }
    ]
  }
}
```

For example, this policy disallows the incoming request:

```
{
  "principalId": "123",
  "policyDocument": {
    "Version": "2012-10-17",
    "Statement": [
      {
        "Action": "execute-api:Invoke",
        "Effect": "Deny",
        "Resource": "arn:aws:execute-api:us-west-2:123456789012:
          ymy8tbxw7b/*/GET/"
      }
    ]
  }
}
```

Given this information, we can create a class structure to be deserialized from Lambda's input event and serialized to JSON. We can start with creating a class named `AuthorizationInput` in order to represent the input event. Let's start with creating a new package for model classes:

```
$ mkdir -p lambda-authorizer/src/main/java/com/serverlessbook/
  lambda/authorizer/models
```

Then, let's create `AuthorizationInput.java` inside it:

```
$ touch lambda-authorizer/src/main/java/com/serverlessbook/
  lambda/authorizer/models/AuthorizationInput.java
```

The content of this class would be as follows:

```
package com.serverlessbook.lambda.authorizer.models;

import com.fasterxml.jackson.annotation.JsonProperty;

public class AuthorizationInput {

    @JsonProperty("authorizationToken")
    private String authorizationToken;

    @JsonProperty("methodArn")
    private String methodArn;

    @JsonProperty("type")
    private String type;

    /**
     * Returns the Authorization token given in the request
     *
     * @return Authorization token
     */
    public String getAuthorizationToken() {
        return authorizationToken.split(" ", 2)[1];
    }

    /**
     * Returns the invoked API Gateway Method's ARN.
     *
     * @return Method ARN
     */
    public String getMethodArn() {
        return methodArn;
    }
```

```
    /**
     * Payload type. Currently the only value is TOKEN
     *
     * @return Payload type
     */
    public String getType() {
        return type;
    }
}
```

This class is self-explanatory; it has three properties marked with Jackson's annotations that allows deserialization from JSON. Also, we added getters for these properties. Note that in getAuthorizationToken, we have a simple logic. That is because we will use **Bearer** tokens. This means that clients will send us authentication tokens in the Authorization header and in the Bearer ACCESS_TOKEN format. This is a pattern introduced in HTTP 1.0 and widely used, so we also use it here. What our getter does here is basically return the token after the Bearer keyword. You can ask this question here: what happens if the incoming token is not complying with the Bearer token pattern? We do not have to worry about it in our Lambda because API Gateway has an option to match the token before it calls the Lambda function, so we can make sure that the incoming data is sanitized.

After the input object, we can create the output model. Let's first create the class file with this command:

```
$ touch lambda-authorizer/src/main/java/com/serverlessbook
    /lambda/authorizer/models/AuthorizationOutput.java
```

This class is a bit more complicated compared to the previous one because it has some nested objects. Let's start with the outer class:

```
package com.serverlessbook.lambda.authorizer.models;

import com.fasterxml.jackson.annotation.JsonGetter;
import com.serverlessbook.lambda.authorizer.models.policy.PolicyDocument;

public class AuthorizationOutput {

    private final String principalId;

    private final PolicyDocument policyDocument;

    public AuthorizationOutput(String principalId, PolicyDocument
policyDocument) {
        this.principalId = principalId;
        this.policyDocument = policyDocument;
    }
```

```java
@JsonGetter("principalId")
public String getPrincipalId() {
    return principalId;
}

@JsonGetter("policyDocument")
public PolicyDocument getPolicyDocument() {
    return policyDocument;
}
}
```

Note that in order to create this object, we require a `PolicyDocument` object. Why not create it now? Let's do that:

```
$ mkdir -p lambda-authorizer/src/main/java/com/serverlessbook/
  lambda/authorizer/models/policy
$ touch lambda-authorizer/src/main/java/com/serverlessbook/
  lambda/authorizer/models/policy/PolicyDocument.java
```

Let's fill in this class with this code:

```java
package com.serverlessbook.lambda.authorizer.models.policy;

import com.fasterxml.jackson.annotation.JsonGetter;
import com.fasterxml.jackson.annotation.JsonIgnore;

import java.util.ArrayList;
import java.util.Collections;
import java.util.List;

public class PolicyDocument {

    private final List<PolicyStatement> policyStatements = new
ArrayList<>();

    @JsonIgnore
    public PolicyDocument withPolicyStatement(PolicyStatement
policyStatement) {
        policyStatements.add(policyStatement);
        return this;
    }

    @JsonGetter("Version")
    public String getVersion() {
        return "2012-10-17";
    }

    @JsonGetter("Statement")
```

```
    public List<PolicyStatement> getPolicyStatements() {
        return Collections.unmodifiableList(policyStatements);
    }
}
```

And finally, let's create the latest nested class, PolicyStatement:

```
$ touch lambda-authorizer/src/main/java/com/serverlessbook/
   lambda/authorizer/models/policy/PolicyStatement.java
```

Let's create the class with the following code:

```java
package com.serverlessbook.lambda.authorizer.models.policy;
import com.fasterxml.jackson.annotation.JsonGetter;
public class PolicyStatement {
    public enum Effect {
        ALLOW("Allow"),
        DENY("Deny");
        private final String effect;
        Effect(String effect) {
            this.effect = effect;
        }
        public String toString() {
            return effect;
        }
    }
    public final String action;
    public final Effect effect;
    public final String resource;
    public PolicyStatement(String action, Effect effect, String resource) {
        this.action = action;
        this.effect = effect;
        this.resource = resource;
    }
    @JsonGetter("Action")
    public String getAction() {
        return action;
    }
    @JsonGetter("Effect")
    public Effect getEffect() {
        return effect;
    }
    @JsonGetter("Resource")
    public String getResource() {
        return resource;
    }
}
```

These classes are nothing special; they are just POJOs with Jackson JSON Library's annotations. If you do not understand the annotations, it is recommended that you refer to the Jackson documentation at `https://github.com/FasterXML/jackson-annotations/wiki/Jackson-An notations`.

Finally, we can write the Lambda function. Let's create the file first:

```
$ touch lambda-authorizer/src/main/java/com/serverlessbook/
  lambda/authorizer/Handler.java
```

As we mentioned in the beginning, this Lambda handler merely reads the incoming token, and if it is equal to `serverless`, it will allow the request. If not, it will return the DENY policy. Let's take a look at the code:

```
package com.serverlessbook.lambda.authorizer.models;

import com.amazonaws.services.lambda.runtime.Context;
import com.serverlessbook.lambda.LambdaHandler;
import com.serverlessbook.lambda.authorizer.models.policy.PolicyDocument;
import com.serverlessbook.lambda.authorizer.models.policy.PolicyStatement;

public class Handler extends LambdaHandler<AuthorizationInput,
AuthorizationOutput> {

  @Override
  public AuthorizationOutput handleRequest(AuthorizationInput input,
Context context){
      final String authenticationToken = input.getAuthorizationToken();
      final PolicyDocument policyDocument = new PolicyDocument();
      final PolicyStatement.Effect policyEffect =
        "serverless".equals(authenticationToken) ?
        PolicyStatement.Effect.ALLOW : PolicyStatement.Effect.DENY;
      policyDocument.withPolicyStatement(new PolicyStatement(
        "execute-api:Invoke", policyEffect, input.getMethodArn()));
      return new AuthorizationOutput("1234", policyDocument);
  }
}
```

In future, this Lambda function will validate the token against an underlying authentication service, but for now, it is very simple.

As a next step, we will modify our CloudFormation template to create a Lambda function using this module, define it as a Lambda authorizer, and bind to our test REST method in order to limit its access only to clients that have the valid token.

We can start with adding the Lambda function to the Resources section of our CloudFormation template. Let's add this block to our template now:

```
"AuthorizerLambda": {
  "Type": "AWS::Lambda::Function",
  "Properties": {
    "Handler": "com.serverlessbook.lambda.authorizer.Handler",
    "Runtime": "java8",
    "Timeout": "300",
    "MemorySize": "1024",
    "Description": "Test lambda",
    "Role": {
      "Fn::GetAtt": [
        "LambdaExecutionRole",
        "Arn"
      ]
    },
    "Code": {
      "S3Bucket": {
        "Ref": "DeploymentBucket"
      },
      "S3Key": {
        "Fn::Sub": "artifacts/lambda- authorizer/
          ${ProjectVersion}/${DeploymentTime}.jar"
      }
    }
  }
}
```

As you may remember from previous sections, this is just another Lambda function, and it does make much difference other than the S3Key and Handler properties.

We should also authorize API Gateway to invoke Lambda functions. We can accomplish this with a little modification of our `LambdaExecutionRole` resource. We should add `apigateway.amazon.aws` to the `Service` section. Take a look at this:

```
"Service": [
    "lambda.amazonaws.com"
]
```

We have to replace the preceding code with the following code:

```
"Service": [
    "lambda.amazonaws.com",
    "apigateway.amazonaws.com"
]
```

After this preparation, we can create the `AWS::ApiGateway::Authorizer` resource to define an authorizer:

```
"ApiGatewayAuthorizer": {
  "Type": "AWS::ApiGateway::Authorizer",
  "Properties": {
    "Name": "AUTHORIZER",
    "Type": "TOKEN",
    "RestApiId": {
      "Ref": "RestApi"
    },
    "AuthorizerUri": {
      "Fn::Sub": "arn:aws:apigateway:${AWS::Region}:lambda:path/
        2015-03-31/functions/${AuthorizerLambda.Arn}/invocations"
    },
    "AuthorizerCredentials": {
      "Fn::GetAtt": [
        "LambdaExecutionRole",
        "Arn"
      ]
    },
    "IdentitySource": "method.request.header.Authorization",
      "IdentityValidationExpression": "Bearer ?[a-zA-Z_0-9+=,.@\\-_/-]+",
      "AuthorizerResultTtlInSeconds": 120
  }
}
```

We must tell the Lambda function to allow invocation by API Gateway:

```
"AuthorizerLambdaPermisson": {
  "Type": "AWS::Lambda::Permission",
    "Properties": {
      "Action": "lambda:InvokeFunction",
      "FunctionName": {
        "Ref": "AuthorizerLambda"
      },
      "Principal": "apigateway.amazonaws.com",
      "SourceArn": {
        "Fn::Sub": "arn:aws:execute-api:${AWS::Region}:
        ${AWS::AccountId}:${RestApi}/authorizers/${ApiGatewayAuthorizer}"
      }
    }
}
```

Finally, we must modify the `TestGetMethod` resource to use the Lambda authorizer. To do that, take a look at the following code:

```
"AuthorizationType": "NONE",
```

We need to replace the preceding code with the following:

```
"AuthorizationType": "CUSTOM",
  "AuthorizerId": {
    "Ref": "ApiGatewayAuthorizer"
},
```

Now, you can deploy the API and see that unless you provide an Authorization header with the `Bearer serverless` value, the request will always fail.

We can try it with Curl and see it in action:

```
$ curl -H "Authorization: Bearer wrong_token"
  https://serverlessbook.example.com/test?value=hello+world
  {"Message":"User is not authorized to access this resource"}
$ curl -H "Authorization: Bearer serverless"
  https://serverlessbook.example.com/test?value=hello+world
  {"value":"hello world"}
```

As you can see, we've managed to build a decoupled authorization system that is usable by as many as functions as we desire.

Summary

In this chapter, we created a serverless REST API with our Lambda function as a backend. We looked at how to configure API Gateway and what options are available for future use cases. We saw that API Gateway lacks some features but it is possible to solve this issue by leveraging CloudFront CDN in front of API Gateway. We configured our custom domain using the Route 53 DNS service and even created a free SSL certificate to use with our CDN. At the end of the chapter, we had a fully serverless and fully AWS-backed REST API. We also spoke a bit about serverless architectures.

This chapter was full of CloudFormation configurations more than actual code. CloudFormation is a sum of all AWS configurations and, obviously, it is a very large topic that we cannot cover fully. If you do not understand some of the options, do not hesitate to refer to the AWS configuration, which includes more specific information about each configuration value.

In the next chapter, we will finally dive into some Java code. We will create a data access layer using serverless and a NoSQL database engine DynamoDB as a data storage layer. We will update our authorizer Lambda to authenticate requests against the DynamoDB table.

4

Applying Enterprise Patterns

Maybe it is possible to build projects with the Java language with a simple code organization, throwing some working code parts and having a just-works project at the end of the day. However, the Java culture is famous for more complicated code structures, abstraction of different layers, creating small, independently testable components, and gluing it all together. Maybe it is not the right name for that, but often, this approach reminds people of **enterprise programming**.

AWS Lambda functions might seem like small, independent functions and they really are. Our colleagues who write Lambda functions with other programming languages, such as Node.JS or Python, tend to put everything into simple functions, often ignoring code reusability and separation of concerns. It is very easy to find Lambda functions consisting of only a single file with all the business logic. However, often our Lambda functions will have complicated business rules and it will be hard to maintain everything in a single file, and if your project consists of more than one Lambda function, you will need a structure to share common logic between functions.

With Java EE or Spring Framework-based projects, we mostly create different modules for different responsibilities of the project, we test them independently from others, and we glue all these components using the **Dependency Injection (DI)** pattern. In a classical Domain Driven Design application, we have the service layer that operates over the objects, the repository layer that is busy with persisting those objects, and a presentation layer that consumes the data coming from underlying layers. The presentation layer is mostly set up as a starting point of the project, and we create a Dependency Injection configuration there to configure other backend layers. The implementation can be different between different projects, but the main principle stays same: underlying layers are not aware who is consuming them; they are just created by the Dependency Injection framework and injected to objects that need them.

In the previous chapter, we started with building our real application and implemented a basic Lambda function that authorizes users using an access token. For a production code, we need some logic to query tokens against a repository, and we need a repository to persist User and Token objects. In future, maybe AWS will release a new database solution and we might need to change the data storage engine. These services will be also needed by other Lambda functions, say, to register a new user or obtain a new token, so they should be reusable. In the worst case scenario, we might need to give up AWS Lambda and replace it with a good old MVC framework. Why change business logic in such a case?

To solve these problems, in this chapter, we will write our first service, User Service, and configure the Dependency Injection framework to make them available to the AWS Lambda function. With a Dependency Injection framework, we will use Google's Guice, a lightweight DI framework that also supports JSR-330 specification.

 JSR-330 is the Java specification that standardizes annotations such as `@Inject` and the `Provider` interfaces for Java platforms. If you use these standardized annotations in your project, you can easily switch to another DI framework that supports these annotations in future.

In this chapter, we will cover the following topics:

- Creating User Service
- Configuring Guice
- Writing the Lambda Handler class with injected dependency
- Adding logging
- Service dependencies

Creating User Service

We will now start implementing our first service, User Service. In the beginning, we will only implement a method that returns a `User` object for a given token string. If a user can't be found in the repository, the method will return `UserNotFoundException`, which should be caught by the AWS Lambda function and translated into the decline policy.

We can start implementing our User Service in the way we already know. Let's add our new module's name to the `settings.gradle` file using a simple echo command:

```
$ echo "include 'services-user'" >> settings.gradle
```

Create the required folder using the following command:

```
$ mkdir -p services-user/src/main/java/com/serverlessbook/services/user
```

It is a good time to create a User object for our project now. The User class will have the ID, email, and username properties, and it will be a POJO. We can create the User object under a new package named domain:

```
$ mkdir -p services-user/src/main/java/com/
  serverlessbook/services/user/domain
```

And we can implement the class as follows:

```java
package com.serverlessbook.services.user.domain;
public class User {

  private int id;
  private String username;
  private String email;
  public int getId() {
    return id;
  }

  public User withId(int id) {
    this.id = id;
    return this;
  }

  public String getUsername() {
    return username;
  }

  public User withUsername(String username) {
    this.username = username;
    return this;
  }

  public String getEmail() {
    return email;
  }
  public User withEmail(String email) {
    this.email = email;
    return this;
  }
}
```

We can now create the interface for `UserService`. Note that `UserService` will be just an interface and other consuming services-in our case, our AWS Lambda function-will be aware of the interface only. However, the Dependency Injection framework will be injecting a concrete implementation of the interface. In this way, you can switch a different implementation of the same service interface, and you can even mock the interface to produce a fake service for unit testing purposes. Preferring interface abstraction over concrete implementations is called **Dependency Inversion Principle** and stands for "**D**" of **SOLID** principles.

Then, we can create the `UserService` class in our new module:

```
package com.serverlessbook.services.user;
import com.serverlessbook.services.user.domain.User;
public interface UserService {
  User getUserByToken(String token) throws UserNotFoundException;
}
```

We must also implement a basic exception class for users not found, and it can also go to the same package:

```
package com.serverlessbook.services.user;
public class UserNotFoundException extends Exception {
  private static final long serialVersionUID = -3235669501483817417L;
}
```

Now we can create the implementation of `UserService`. In the beginning, our concrete method will throw `UserNotFoundException`:

```
package com.serverlessbook.services.user;
import com.serverlessbook.services.user.domain.User;
public class UserServiceImpl implements UserService {
  @Override
  public User getUserByToken(String token) throws UserNotFoundException {
    throw new UserNotFoundException();
  }
}
```

We keep it simple for now because without the data layer, it does not make any sense to write more business logic. However, at this stage, we are ready to consume this service in our AWS Lambda and see it in action.

Configuring Guice

To configure Guice, we must first add it as a dependency. We will add the Guice dependency independently to AWS Lambda functions, but it is also a good idea to have version information somewhere in the main project. That's why we export the `guiceVersion` variable from the parent project's `build.gradle` file first:

```
ext {
  guiceVersion = '4.1.+'
}
```

Now we can add Guice's dependency to the `lambda-authorizer` module's dependencies. Here, we did not create any `build.gradle` file, so let's create it first:

$ touch lambda-authorizer/build.gradle

The, let's add the following content:

```
dependencies {
  compile group: 'com.google.inject', name: 'guice', version: guiceVersion
}
```

At this step, it is also convenient to add the `services-user` project as a dependency to this Lambda function. So, we can add also this line to the dependencies:

```
compile project(':services-user')
```

Now we can go on to creating a dependency injection configuration. Guice provides an `AbstractModule` class to configure dependencies. For each Lambda function, we must create a class deriving from `AbstractModule`, and in that class, we can define our dependencies. Now we can start with creating this class with the following command:

$ touch lambda-authorizer/src/main/java/com/serverlessbook/ lambda/authorizer/DependencyInjectionModule.java

Let's add this content to this class:

```
package com.serverlessbook.lambda.authorizer;
import com.google.inject.AbstractModule;
public class DependencyInjectionModule extends AbstractModule {
  @Override
  protected void configure() {
  }
}
```

`configure()` is an abstract method that must be implemented for every child class, and inside this method, you can create bindings like the following:

```
@Override
protected void configure() {
    bind(UserService.class).to(UserServiceImpl.class);
}
```

It is the simplest dependency declaration method, which tells Guice to return an instance of `UserServiceImpl` whenever it is needed in any class.

Now let's see how we can use Guice in our Handler class.

Writing the Lambda Handler class with injected dependency

The Handler class is the entrance point for our project because AWS Lambda runtime calls it first. You already know that AWS will invoke the `handleRequest` method for each invocation of Lambda function. To create the object, Lambda runtime uses the default constructor of the class where the Handler is. So, to inject dependencies to our class, we will use this knowledge and initiate the injection when the default constructor is called. Moreover, Lambda runtime will keep a cached copy of an object once it is initiated and shared among different invocations of your Lambda function. It means that the injection will not happen for every invocation and, although we cannot predict when a new instance of Handler class will be created, will be cached.

We can start adding a Guice injector as a static field in the `Handler` class:

```
public class Handler extends LambdaHandler<AuthorizationInput,
AuthorizationOutput> {

   private static final Injector INJECTOR = Guice.createInjector(new
      DependencyInjectionModule());
   @Override
   public AuthorizationOutput handleRequest(AuthorizationInput input,
Context context) {
      .....
   }
}
```

Now we can add a `UserService` field to our Handler class and its setter:

```
private UserService userService;
```

```
@Inject
public void setUserService(UserService userService) {
  this.userService = userService;
}
```

Here, note the `@Inject` annotation usage. It is a **JSR-330** annotation, which indicates that `UserService` is needed as a dependency in the Handler class. But putting this annotation alone does not trigger its execution, so we must tell Guice to evaluate the `javax.inject` annotations and provide the dependencies. In order to achieve this result, we must create a default constructor for our `Handler()` method and add the following directive there:

```
public Handler() {
  INJECTOR.injectMembers(this);
  Objects.requireNonNull(userService);
}
```

Note that we added the `Objects.requireNonNull` check just after the `injectMembers` call. This ensures that the dependency is injected. At this step, even before we deploy the code to AWS Runtime, we can write a Junit test and see that DI is working. Let us see how to do that:

1. Let's create the test file:

    ```
    $ touch lambda-authorizer/src/test/java/com/serverlessbook/
      lambda/authorizer/HandlerTest.java
    ```

2. We will write the test now:

    ```
    package com.serverlessbook.lambda.authorizer;
    import org.junit.Test;
    public class HandlerTest {
      @Test
       public void testDependencies() throws Exception {
          Handler testHandler = new Handler();
      }
    }
    ```

3. Let's execute the test:

    ```
    $ ./gradlew test
    ```

We see that it passes. You can play with the handler code, for example, removing the `@Inject` annotation and seeing that the test fails.

Now, given that we have `UserService` injected into our Handler, we can finally modify the `handleRequest` method to consume this service. This method will receive the authorization token input from API Gateway, authorize it against the service and return the result:

```
@Override
public AuthorizationOutput handleRequest(AuthorizationInput input, Context
context) {
  final String authenticationToken = input.getAuthorizationToken();
  final PolicyDocument policyDocument = new PolicyDocument();
  PolicyStatement.Effect policyEffect = PolicyStatement.Effect.ALLOW;
  String principalId = null;

  try {
    User authenticatedUser =
userService.getUserByToken(authenticationToken);
    principalId = String.valueOf(authenticatedUser.getId());
  } catch (UserNotFoundException userNotFoundException) {
    policyEffect = PolicyStatement.Effect.DENY;
  }

  policyDocument.withPolicyStatement(new PolicyStatement("execute-
api:Invoke",
      policyEffect, input.getMethodArn()));
  return new AuthorizationOutput(principalId, policyDocument);
}
```

Adding logging

We should also log when there is an authentication issue. Let's add a Logger to our Handler class:

```
private static final Logger LOGGER =
  Logger.getLogger(Handler.class);
```

Then, let's modify the block where we catch the exception:

```
...
  } catch (UserNotFoundException userNotFoundException) {
    policyEffect = PolicyStatement.Effect.DENY;
    LOGGER.info("User authentication failed for token " +
      authenticationToken);
  }
....
```

Maybe at this point, we can create another test to check whether our Handler class is returning the denial policy. We need mocking for that because we will create a mock `AuthenticationInput` object, and easymock and powermock are good libraries for that. Let's add it to our main `build.gradle` file to test dependencies:

```
allprojects {
  dependencies {
    ...
    testCompile group: 'org.easymock', 'name': 'easymock',
      'version': '3.4'
    testCompile group: 'org.powermock', name:
      'powermock-mockito-release-full', version: '1.5.+', ext: 'pom'
  }
}
```

Then, we can add a new test to the `HandlerTest` class:

```
@Test
public void testFailingToken() throws Exception {
  Handler testHandler = new Handler();
  AuthorizationInput mockEvent =
    createNiceMock(AuthorizationInput.class);
  expect(mockEvent.getAuthorizationToken()).andReturn("
    INVALID_TOKEN").anyTimes();
  replay(mockEvent);

  AuthorizationOutput authorizationOutput =
    testHandler.handleRequest(mockEvent, null);
  assertEquals(PolicyStatement.Effect.DENY,
    authorizationOutput.getPolicyDocument().
    getPolicyStatements().get(0).getEffect());
}
```

Running the test should succeed because for any tokens, we return `PolicyStatement.Effect.DENY` from the `handleRequest` method.

Service dependencies

Often, the services we declare have other dependencies. For example, our user service needs a repository service to access the persistence layer. How do we declare these nested dependencies and get the Guice construct to the dependency graph for us?

We can leverage JSR-330 annotations again to declare dependencies for other dependencies. As always, let's look at this in action. Let's start with creating the UserRepository interface in the com.serverlessbook.services.user.repository package:

```
$ mkdir -p services-user/src/main/java/com/
  serverlessbook/services/user/repository
$ touch services-user/src/main/java/com/serverlessbook/
  services/user/repository/UserRepository.java
```

Inside the interface, let's declare the method we need at this stage:

```
package com.serverlessbook.services.user.repository;
import com.serverlessbook.services.user.domain.User;
import java.util.Optional;
public interface UserRepository {
    Optional<User> getUserByToken(String token);
}
```

Then, let's create a nonfunctional implementation of this class with the name UserRepositoryDynamoDB:

```
package com.serverlessbook.services.user.repository;
import com.serverlessbook.services.user.domain.User;
import java.util.Optional;
public class UserRepositoryDynamoDB implements UserRepository {
    @Override
    public Optional<User> getUserByToken(String token) {
      return Optional.empty();
    }
}
```

This class always returns an empty User object because at this stage, we do not need the real implementation. We will be implementing the real data layer in the next chapter.

Now we can add UserRepositoryDynamoDB as a dependency to the UserServiceImpl class. Let's add a private field to the UserServiceImpl class and create a constructor for it:

```
private final UserRepository userRepository;
public UserServiceImpl(UserRepository userRepository) {
    this.userRepository = userRepository;
    Objects.requireNonNull(userRepository);
}
```

At this step, executing tests again will end up failing because Guice cannot create UserServiceImpl without a zero-argument constructor in this configuration. Actually, the Guice error explains the problem and provides a clue about the solution:

Could not find a suitable constructor in
`com.serverlessbook.services.user.UserServiceImpl`. Classes must have either one
(and only one) constructor annotated with `@Inject` or a zero-argument constructor that is
not private.

Then, we must use two steps to complete the puzzle here:

1. Add the `@Inject` annotation to the constructor so that Guice will understand
   that it should construct the object using this constructor, injecting the required
   parameters to it.
2. Declare `UserRepositoryDynamoDB` as the implementation of `UserRepository`.

To benefit from JSR-330 annotations, the `javax.inject:javax.inject` Maven package is
sufficient. We can apply it to all subprojects in our parent `build.gradle` file:

```
allprojects {
  dependencies {
    compileOnly group: 'javax.inject', name: 'javax.inject', version: '1'
    ...
  }
}
```

Note that we used the `compileOnly` directive for this dependency. This is
because Guice is already including this dependency as a compile
dependency. Therefore, for other subprojects, it is just an optional
dependency. If we compile our service subprojects independently, we do
not need to add JSR-330 annotations in our JAR package because they are
not consumed by this project itself. If Guice requires these packages, it
already has those classes in a compiled form. We can then declare these
annotations as a compile-only dependency, and it will simplify our Gradle
dependency graph.

As we have JSR-330 annotations in our project, we can now mark the constructor with the
`@Inject` annotation:

```
@Inject
public UserServiceImpl(UserRepository userRepository) {
    this.userRepository = userRepository;
    Objects.requireNonNull(userRepository);
}
```

We can also make the `getUserByToken` method use the repository:

```
@Override
public User getUserByToken(String token) throws UserNotFoundException {
  return
userRepository.getUserByToken(token).orElseThrow(UserNotFoundException::new
);
}
```

If we run the test now, we will see that Guice is complaining because of another issue. You can see the error message as follows:

```
No implementation for com.serverlessbook.services.user.
   repository.UserRepository was bound.  while locating
   com.serverlessbook.services.user.repository.UserRepository
```

We can solve this error by declaring `UserRepositoryDynamoDB` as the implementation of the `UserRepository` class in `DependencyInjectionModule`:

```
@Override
protected void configure() {
   bind(UserService.class).to(UserServiceImpl.class);
   bind(UserRepository.class).to(UserRepositoryDynamoDB.class);
}
```

Now you will see that our test passes because Guice can locate all the dependencies and inject them wherever they are needed.

In this chapter, we never deployed the application; now, we can deploy it and see whether the "serverless" token is accepted as a valid token:

```
$ curl -H "Authorization: Bearer serverless"
   https://serverlessbook.merkurapp.com/test?value=hello+world
   {"Message":"User is not authorized to access this resource"}
```

So far, so good. Now different parts of our application are decoupled. We will be using DynamoDB as a data storage layer, but if we need to change it to another data storage engine, we will not touch our Lambda handler, and changing only one line in the DI configuration will be sufficient.

Summary

In this chapter, we explored how to configure the Dependency Injection pattern in the AWS Lambda environment. Our authenticator Lambda is now relying on underlying services that will be shared between different Lambda functions. Our Data Access Layer is not connected to any data storage engine still, so in the next chapter, we will introduce DynamoDB for that and see how we can map Java objects to DynamoDB tables.

5
Persisting Data

So far in our book, we've introduced many important concepts about how to think in serverless environments, and we explored the fundamentals. In this chapter, we will implement a vast majority of our example forum application, endpoints for user creation, post creation and reading, and more importantly, we will persist our data in a data storage layer. The data storage engine we picked for this project is DynamoDB, the schemaless database engine of AWS. In this long chapter, we will cover the following topics:

- Creating DynamoDB tables using CloudFormation
- Injecting environment variables to Lambda functions
- Creating endpoints with more sophisticated input and output types

Introduction to DynamoDB

As the AWS documentation states, Amazon DynamoDB is a fully managed NoSQL database service that provides fast and predictable performance with seamless scalability. With AmazonDB, you do not need to worry about the administrative aspects of a database engine; you create tables, define indexes to be used to search the data, and use it with SDKs available to many programming languages. DynamoDB tables can scale up and scale down as you need; the only thing you have to do is adjust the reserved throughput capacity.

In DynamoDB, you work with tables, items, and attributes. Let's briefly explain these concepts:

- **Tables**: Similar to other database systems, DynamoDB stores data in different tables. For example, we will have three tables, `Tokens`, `Users`, and `Threads`, which will store three different data types.
- **Items**: Items are like rows in relational database systems. Every table consists of practically an unlimited size of items. For example, every user in the `Users` table is an item.
- **Attributes**: Each item consists of one or more attributes. Attributes can be primitive data types or nested JSON documents. Except indexed attributes, DynamoDB tables do not dictate any data structure, so you can populate your table with different type of attributes.

A very important concept of DynamoDB is indexing, or keys in the DynamoDB terminology. Keys help the DynamoDB engine place items into physical locations and also plays an important role when the user wants to search data by keys. Upon creating a new DynamoDB table, you must specify an attribute as the primary key. Primary keys are used to distinguish different items and also provide the physical location of the item for the DynamoDB internal engine. There are two types of primary keys:

- **Partition key**: The Partition Index is the principal index that every item must have. DynamoDB uses the Partition Index to determine the physical location of the item. Practically, it can be considered the primary index in an RDBMS. Let's assume that we have a `Users` table; then, the `UserId` attribute is a good candidate for a Partition Index.
- **Partition key and sort key**: In this type of key, you define two attributes as members of the key; first, the partition key and second the sort key. Items with the same partition keys go to the same physical location and the sort key can be used to query data in conjunction with the partition key. As an example, in a table that stores forum posts, `threadId` can be the partition key while the date attribute is a sort key.

 The partition key is also known as **hash key**, while the sort key is known as the **range key**. You will see this wording in AWS SDK in the following sections.

DynamoDB also provides a second type of indexes, which are called **secondary indexes**. DynamoDB supports two types of secondary indexes:

- **Global secondary index**: This is an index with a partition key and a sort key that can be different from those on the base table. A global secondary index is considered "global" because queries on the index can span all of the data in the base table across all partitions.
- **Local secondary index**: This is an index that has the same partition key as the base table but a different sort key. A local secondary index is "local" in the sense that every partition of a local secondary index is scoped to a base table partition that has the same partition key value.

There are some key differences between these two types of indexes. For example, local secondary indexes can be created in conjunction with primary keys, while global secondary indexes can be created independently from them.

At this point, it is also convenient to mention the scalability of DynamoDB. DynamoDB has practically infinite scalability, and the read/write capacity that provides it is determined by the provisioned throughput setting you configure per table. In DynamoDB, you specify provisioned throughput requirements in terms of capacity units. One read capacity unit represents one strongly consistent read per second, or two eventually consistent reads per second, for items up to 4 KB in size. One write capacity unit represents one write per second for items up to 1 KB in size. You should calculate the approximate capacity required for your use case and configure it per table, and DynamoDB will guarantee that it will provide this capacity. AWS charges you per throughput capacity you purchased. Even if you do not use the purchased capacity, you are always charged as long as your table is live. Therefore, you should constantly monitor your DynamoDB usage and adjust your purchased throughput capacity for cost saving. There is an important point about throughput and secondary indexes: local secondary indexes use the reserved capacity for the table, while you must purchase separate throughput capacity for global secondary indexes. That's why you should analyze your indexing needs and avoid creating so many global secondary indexes.

You can refer to the AWS documentation for a deeper discussion on DynamoDB while we go on with the practical aspects of the topic.

Creating the first table

In the previous chapter, we created an API authorizer that does not have any underlying data layer. Now we will create two DynamoDB tables, which are User and Token tables. As per their names, these tables will store our user list and access tokens, respectively.

Now let's add this block to our CloudFormation template's Resources section in order to create our UserTable table:

```
"UserTable": {
  "Type": "AWS::DynamoDB::Table",
  "Properties": {
    "AttributeDefinitions": [
      {
        "AttributeName": "UserId",
        "AttributeType": "S"
      }
    ],
    "KeySchema": [
      {
        "AttributeName": "UserId",
        "KeyType": "HASH"
      }
    ],
    "ProvisionedThroughput": {
      "ReadCapacityUnits": 1,
      "WriteCapacityUnits": 1
    }
  }
}
```

If we analyze the definition, we can see that we define the UserId attribute as S, which means string. This might seem surprising and you might ask why we do not use numeric values. Our UserId will be a UUID format (such as 123e4567-e89b-12d3-a456-426655440000) because in DynamoDB, there is no way to create auto-increment values. Therefore, generating random UUIDs in the string format is a better option. In previous chapters, when we created a User object, the Id property was also a string.

You might also ask why we only define the UserId attribute's type?

That's because DynamoDB forces us to define the types of attributes we use in keys. For the User table, we have only one primary key represented by UserId; therefore, we must define its type. We are free to add more attributes to this table, but we are not forced to define them upon table creation. In the KeySchema section, we define UserId as the hash key, so it becomes a unique key for every user.

For the `UserTable` table, we do not need any secondary indexes, so we skip it for now.

The `ProvisionedThroughput` property lets us define the purchased throughput value, which we set as 1 for now for both reads and writes. For production applications, you would consider increasing this value according to your needs.

Creating the second table for access tokens

Before we deploy the stack and create the first table, it is a good idea to create the second table, which will store access tokens:

This table will store `UserId` and `Token` values, and the primary index will be the `Token` value:

```
"TokenTable": {
  "Type": "AWS::DynamoDB::Table",
  "Properties": {
    "AttributeDefinitions": [
      {
        "AttributeName": "Token",
        "AttributeType": "S"
      }
    ],
    "KeySchema": [
      {
        "AttributeName": "Token",
        "KeyType": "HASH"
      }
    ],
    "ProvisionedThroughput": {
      "ReadCapacityUnits": 1,
      "WriteCapacityUnits": 1
    }
  }
}
```

After creating both tables, we have to modify our `LambdaPolicy` to allow access to these tables. Let's replace the `LambdaCustomPolicy` resource with the following block:

```
"LambdaCustomPolicy": {
  "Type": "AWS::IAM::Policy",
  "Properties": {
    "PolicyName": "LambdaCustomPolicy",
    "PolicyDocument": {
      "Version": "2012-10-17",
```

```
        "Statement": [
          {
            "Effect": "Allow",
            "Action": [
              "dynamodb:BatchGetItem",
              "dynamodb:BatchWriteItem",
              "dynamodb:DeleteItem",
              "dynamodb:GetItem",
              "dynamodb:GetRecords",
              "dynamodb:GetShardIterator",
              "dynamodb:ListTables",
              "dynamodb:PutItem",
              "dynamodb:Query",
              "dynamodb:Scan",
              "dynamodb:UpdateItem"
            ],
            "Resource": [
              {
                "Fn::Sub": "arn:aws:dynamodb:${AWS::Region}:
                  ${AWS::AccountId}:table/${TokenTable}*"
              },
              {
                "Fn::Sub": "arn:aws:dynamodb:${AWS::Region}:
                  ${AWS::AccountId}:table/${UserTable}*"
              }
            ]
          }
        ]
      },
      "Roles": [
        {
          "Ref": "LambdaExecutionRole"
        }
      ]
    }
  }
```

What we did here was allow our Lambda function to operate read and write operations on
User and Token tables. When we add more tables in future, we will add those table names
to the IAM policy.

After we create our tables, we can finally start writing some Java code. As a first step, we will create a new module, which is called `repository-dynamodb`, which will include some common functionality for every service that uses DynamoDB as the data layer. As we are already familiar with how we create a new module, we can repeat the same process again:

```
$ mkdir -p repository-dynamodb/src/main/java/
   com/serverlessbook/repository
$ echo "include 'repository-dynamodb'" >> settings.gradle
```

Now under the new module, we should create a new `build.gradle` file and add the DynamoDB SDK to this module:

```
dependencies {
   compile group: 'com.amazonaws', name: 'aws-java-sdk-dynamodb',
      version: awsSdkVersion}
```

Obviously, this won't work because `awsSdkVersion` was not defined in our project. That's why we also have to edit our main `build.gradle` file to add the `awsSdkVersion` variable:

```
ext {
   guiceVersion = '4.1.+'
   awsSdkVersion = '1.11.+'
}
```

As you might have understood, this will ensure that the DynamoDB SDK is also included with all service modules, which includes the `repository-dynamodb` module.

Now let's create a `build.gradle` file for our user service and add this new module as a dependency to the user service. Let's create the `build.gradle` file first:

```
$ touch services/build.gradle
```

And then let's add `repository-dynamodb` as a dependency into that file:

```
dependencies {
   compile project(':repository-dynamodb')
}
```

Now, the user service is aware of the DynamoDB SDK, so it can use the DynamoDB features.

Configuring the DynamoDB data mapper

The DynamoDB SDK provides a very nice object mapping feature exclusively for Java. It is very similar to JPA and provides a set of annotations to map plain Java objects to DynamoDB records. For our project, we will use this mapper, which makes it much easier to read and write data on DynamoDB. This mapper comes bundled with the DynamoDB SDK, so we do not have to add any other dependency at this moment. Now let's create a new object, Token, which will fill our `Token` table and decorate it with DynamoDB mapping annotations. First, let's create a new file under the `com.serverlessbook.services.user.domain` package:

```
$ touch services-user/src/main/java/com/serverlessbook/
  services/user/domain/Token.java
```

And then let's create this class with the following content:

```
package com.serverlessbook.services.user.domain;
public class Token {
    private String token;
    private String userId;
    public String getToken() {
       return token;
    }
    public void setToken(String token) {
      this.token = token;
    }
    public String getUserId() {
      return userId;
    }
    public void setUserId(String userId) {
      this.userId = userId;
    }
}
```

Now let's look at how we can map these two properties to DynamoDB columns. Let's modify our class as follows:

```
package com.serverlessbook.services.user.domain;
import com.amazonaws.services.dynamodbv2.datamodeling.DynamoDBAttribute;
import com.amazonaws.services.dynamodbv2.datamodeling.DynamoDBHashKey;
public class Token {
  @DynamoDBHashKey(attributeName = "Token")
  private String token;
  @DynamoDBAttribute(attributeName = "UserId")
  private String userId;
  public String getToken() {
    return token;
```

```
    }
    public void setToken(String token) {
        this.token = token;
    }
    public String getUserId() {
        return userId;
    }
    public void setUserId(String userId) {
        this.userId = userId;
    }
}
```

As can be seen, these annotations are marking our Java properties to DynamoDB attributes. Note that the token attribute is marked with `DynamoDBHashKey` because it is our primary key for this table.

You might have noted that in this annotation, we did not have to specify the table name, such as the `@Table` annotation of JPA. Actually, there is a annotation in DynamoDB, which is called `@DynamoDBTable`. However, this annotation expects the table names be hardcoded, which is not suitable for our use case. This is because our CloudFormation template generates the table name using random strings. It is also possible to use hardcoded names for tables in CloudFormation and use those names with the `@DynamoDBTable` annotation. However, for our example project, we wanted to show how to use dynamic table names. To provide dynamic table names, we will inject table names as the environment variable to Lambda functions, and we will configure the DynamoDB client to use these environment variables to resolve table names for every object.

Configuring environment variables for Lambda

We can implement this functionality in the `repository-dynamodb` module now. First of all, we have to remind you that all DynamoDB operations are carried out by an instance of `com.amazonaws.services.dynamodbv2.datamodeling.DynamoDBMapper`. This class is extendable and configurable. One of the configurations is a table name resolver class that implements the `com.amazonaws.services.dynamodbv2.datamodeling.DynamoDBMapperConfig.Tab leNameResolver` interface. What we are going to do is create a child class for DynamoDBMapper, configure it with our own table resolver, `EnvironmentVariableTableNameResolver`, and inject our own implementation of DynamoDBMapper wherever we need an instance of DynamoDBMapper.

We can first start with creating `EnvironmentVariableTableNameResolver`. Let's create this class in the `repository-dynamodb` module:

> **$ touch repository-dynamodb/src/main/java/com/serverlessbook/**
> **repository/EnvironmentVariableTableNameResolver.java**

Let's implement this class, as follows:

```
package com.serverlessbook.repository;
import com.amazonaws.services.dynamodbv2.datamodeling.DynamoDBMapperConfig;
import com.amazonaws.services.dynamodbv2.datamodeling.DynamoDBMapperConfig.
  TableNameResolver;
import
com.amazonaws.services.dynamodbv2.datamodeling.DynamoDBMappingException;
public class EnvironmentVariableTableNameResolver implements
TableNameResolver {
  @Override
  public String getTableName(Class<?> clazz, DynamoDBMapperConfig config){
    String environmentVariableName = "DynamoDb" + clazz.getSimpleName() +
      "Table";
    String tableName = System.getenv(environmentVariableName);
    if (tableName == null) {
      throw new DynamoDBMappingException("DynamoDB table name for " + clazz
+ " cannot be determined. " + environmentVariableName + " environment
variable should be set.");
    }
    return tableName;
  }
}
```

As you can understand, this method gets the class name and returns the DynamoDB table name. In our case, we search for an environment variable in the `DynamoDbCLASS_NAMETable` format. For example, for the `Token` class, our environment variable should be `DynamoDbTokenTable`. In case of an unsolved class, we fail fast and throw an exception. In the following sections, we will provide these environment variables via CloudFormation to Lambda functions.

Now we can implement the custom DynamoDBMapper, which will use the previous table name resolver. Let's create the file:

```
$ touch repository-dynamodb/src/main/java/com/
    serverlessbook/repository/DynamoDBMapperWithCustomTableName.java
```

And then let's implement it with the following content:

```java
package com.serverlessbook.repository;
import com.amazonaws.services.dynamodbv2.AmazonDynamoDBClient;
import com.amazonaws.services.dynamodbv2.datamodeling.DynamoDBMapper;
import com.amazonaws.services.dynamodbv2.datamodeling.
    DynamoDBMapperConfig;
import javax.inject.Inject;

public class DynamoDBMapperWithCustomTableName extends DynamoDBMapper {
    @Inject
    public DynamoDBMapperWithCustomTableName(AmazonDynamoDBClient
        amazonDynamoDBClient) {
        this(amazonDynamoDBClient, new EnvironmentVariableTableNameResolver());
    }
    public DynamoDBMapperWithCustomTableName(AmazonDynamoDBClient
        amazonDynamoDBClient,
        DynamoDBMapperConfig.TableNameResolver tableNameResolver) {
        super(amazonDynamoDBClient, DynamoDBMapperConfig
        .builder()
        .withTableNameResolver(tableNameResolver)
        .build());
    }
}
```

To define a dependency injection bean using this new class, let's open the DependencyInjectionModule class in our authorization Lambda and add this definition:

```java
@Override
protected void configure() {
    //other definitions
    bind(DynamoDBMapper.class).to(DynamoDBMapperWithCustomTableName.class);
}
```

This ensures that whenever an instance of DynamoDBMapper is required by the dependency class, an instance of DynamoDBMapperWithCustomTableName is created and injected to the requiring class.

Now we can inject this newly created dependency to our `UserRepositoryDynamoDB` class, which resides in the `services-user` module. Let's replace the content of this class with the following content:

```
package com.serverlessbook.services.user.repository;

import com.amazonaws.services.dynamodbv2.datamodeling.DynamoDBMapper;
import com.serverlessbook.services.user.domain.User;
import javax.inject.Inject;
import java.util.Optional;

public class UserRepositoryDynamoDB implements UserRepository {
  private final DynamoDBMapper dynamoDBMapper;

  @Inject
  public UserRepositoryDynamoDB(DynamoDBMapper dynamoDBMapper) {
    this.dynamoDBMapper = dynamoDBMapper;
  }

  @Override
  public Optional<User> getUserByToken(String token) {
    return Optional.empty();
  }
}
```

Now we have the necessary dependency to query the token in DynamoDB. Just before we implement this functionality, let's also annotate the `User` class with DynamoDB annotations. Let's replace the content of the `User` class with the following code:

```
package com.serverlessbook.services.user.domain;

import com.amazonaws.services.dynamodbv2.datamodeling.DynamoDBAttribute;
import com.amazonaws.services.dynamodbv2.datamodeling.DynamoDBHashKey;

public class User {

  @DynamoDBHashKey(attributeName = "UserId")
  private String id;

  @DynamoDBAttribute(attributeName = "Username")
  private String username;

  @DynamoDBAttribute(attributeName = "EMail")
  private String email;

  public String getId() {
    return id;
```

```
  }

  public User withId(String id) {
    this.id = id;
    return this;
  }

  public String getUsername() {
    return username;
  }

  public User withUsername(String username) {
    this.username = username;
    return this;
  }

  public String getEmail() {
    return email;
  }

  public User withEmail(String email) {
    this.email = email;
    return this;
  }
}
```

Now, with all the preparations done, we can implement the getUserByToken method in the UserRepositoryDynamoDB class:

```
@Override
public Optional<User> getUserByToken(String token) {
  Token foundTokenInDynamoDB = dynamoDBMapper.load(Token.class, token);
  if (foundTokenInDynamoDB != null) {
    // Token found in DynamoDb, try to fetch the user in a second query
    return Optional.ofNullable(dynamoDBMapper.load(User.class,
      foundTokenInDynamoDB.getUserId()));
  }
  // Token not found, return empty.
  return Optional.empty();
}
```

Here, we fire two DynamoDB queries, but thanks to the DynamoDB mapping features, exclusive to Java, we do not deal with DynamoDB internals that much.

As you may remember, we already had our handler using this service to query the token. We also had a test named com.serverlessbook.lambda.authorizer.HandlerTest, which tests whether an invalid token fails. After the latest modifications, if we run the test using the ./gradlew test command, we will see the following output stating that the test is failing:

```
: lambda-test:compileJava
: lambda-test:classes
: lambda-test:compileTestJava UP-TO-DATE
: lambda-test:testClasses UP-TO-DATE
: lambda-test:test UP-TO-DATE
: lambda-authorizer:classes
: lambda-authorizer:compileTestJava
: lambda-authorizer:testClasses
: lambda-authorizer:test

com.serverlessbook.lambda.authorizer.HandlerTest > testFailingToken FAILED
    com.amazonaws.services.dynamodbv2.datamodeling.DynamoDBMappingException at HandlerTest.java:27

2 tests completed, 1 failed
: lambda-authorizer:test FAILED

FAILURE: Build failed with an exception.
```

This is because our table name resolver is seeking DynamoDB table names in environment variables, which we will inject to Lambda function. To enable our test passing again, we have to give these environment variables to a locally running JVM. Passing environment variables using Gradle is easy, but the challenging part is to find table names in the CloudFormation template and populate environment variables using that. We will have to write some Gradle scripts for this purpose.

First, let's open our main build.gradle file and add this function to the end:

```
import com.amazonaws.auth.DefaultAWSCredentialsProviderChain
import com.amazonaws.regions.Region
import com.amazonaws.regions.Regions
import com.amazonaws.services.cloudformation.AmazonCloudFormationClient
import
com.amazonaws.services.cloudformation.model.DescribeStackResourcesRequest

def getDynamoDbTableNamesFromCloudformationStack(stackName) {
  return Region.getRegion(Regions.fromName(aws.region))
  .createClient(AmazonCloudFormationClient.class, new
  DefaultAWSCredentialsProviderChain(), null)
  .describeStackResources(new
DescribeStackResourcesRequest().withStackName(stackName))
```

```
    .getStackResources().findAll { stackResource ->
stackResource.getResourceType() ==
    "AWS::DynamoDB::Table" }
}
```

This function leverages AWS SDK (which is also available in Gradle itself) to scan all the resources created in a CloudFormation stack and filters all DynamoDB tables created within that stack.

 Note the beauty of the Groovy language. Thanks to Groovy, programming for JVM is a bit easier.

Now we can add the code to use outputs of this function and set environment variables using it. At the end of the `build.gradle` file, add the following block:

```
subprojects {
  test {
    getDynamoDbTableNamesFromCloudformationStack(cloudFormation.
      stackName).each {
      environment 'DynamoDb' + it.getLogicalResourceId(),
        it.getPhysicalResourceId()
    }
  }
}
```

As you may have noted, this code is using the logical resource ID of the stack resource to construct the name of the environment variable. Remember that in the CloudFormation template, we created two tables with `UserTable` and `TokenTable` names. This function, thus, creates two environment variables with `DynamoDbUserTable` and `DynamoDbTokenTable` names and sets their values to physical table names, created randomly by AWS.

Now we can execute the tests again, and we will see that they pass.

The next step will be to add these environment variables to Lambda using CloudFormation. The `AWS::Lambda::Function` resource type has an `Environment` attribute for this purpose. Let's edit our `AuthorizerLambda` now and add environment variables to the Lambda function:

```
"AuthorizerLambda": {
  "Type": "AWS::Lambda::Function",
  "Properties": {
    .
    .
```

```
      .
    "Environment": {
      "Variables": {
        "DynamoDbTokenTable": {
          "Ref": "TokenTable"
        },
        "DynamoDbUserTable": {
          "Ref": "UserTable"
        }
      }
    }
  }
}
```

Now we can deploy the application and give a try to access our API:

```
$ curl -H "Authorization: Bearer serverless"
https://serverlessbook.example.com/test? value=hello+world
{"Message":"User is not authorized to access this resource"}
```

This is an unexpected result because now, our application is seeking the token in DynamoDB and blocking the access because this token does not exist in the table. In the next section, we will be adding user registration and token endpoints, but can we manually add this token and a test user and see that our authorizer works properly? Sure. We can use AWS CLI to add the necessary records and see the result. You can use the following two commands to create a test user and a token for that user:

```
$ aws dynamodb put-item \
    --region us-east-1 \
    --table-name serverlessbook-UserTable-1J77C8QJV8UJA  \
    --item '{"UserId": {"S": "1234-1234-1234-1234"},
      "Username": {"S": "Test User"},
      "EMail": {"S": "test@test.com"}}'

$ aws dynamodb put-item \
    --region us-east-1 \
    --table-name serverlessbook-TokenTable-14B7FBB85X1TB \
    --item '{"UserId": {"S": "1234-1234-1234-1234"},
      "Token": {"S": "serverless"}}'
```

Table names will be different for everybody, so you should go to the AWS console to see the randomly created table names, or you can use AWS CLI to query the stack. After adding the records, check again, using AWS CLI, whether they are correctly added to the tables. Now you can try to access the API again:

```
$ curl -H "Authorization: Bearer serverless"
  https://serverlessbook.merkurapp.com/test?value=hello+world
  {"value":"hello world"}
```

Neat! Now we have a working authentication system without any servers and database systems to maintain.

User registration

In this section, we will be adding the user registration feature to our application. First of all, we have to consider some constraints for our application:

- Only one unique email address can be registered per user
- Every user must have an unique username
- Email addresses must be valid

If one of the checks fails, we have to reject the request. For the first two checks, we have to return the 409 Conflict HTTP code, while for the latest one, we have to return 400 Bad Request. API Gateway uses exceptions for status code. This means that our handler should return exceptions for every case, so we can map those exceptions to HTTP error code on the API Gateway level.

From a business logic point of view, the last requirement is easy; we can add a basic regular expression to check the validity of the email address given by the client. On the other hand, for the first two checks, we have to go to our database and check the existing records. The problem at this stage is that we did not create indexes for the Username and Email attributes, so at the moment, the only way is to scan tables, which is a pretty expensive operation, especially for large tables. Then, before we start adding our business logic, we have to modify our table and create indexes for the Username and Email attributes.

Now let's replace `UserTable` with the following block, which adds `UsernameIndex` as **Global Secondary Index (GSI)**:

```
"UserTable": {
  "Type": "AWS::DynamoDB::Table",
  "Properties": {
    "AttributeDefinitions": [
      {
        "AttributeName": "UserId",
        "AttributeType": "S"
      },
      {
        "AttributeName": "Username",
        "AttributeType": "S"
      }
    ],
    "KeySchema": [
      {
        "AttributeName": "UserId",
        "KeyType": "HASH"
      }
    ],
    "GlobalSecondaryIndexes": [
      {
        "IndexName": "UsernameIndex",
        "KeySchema": [
          {
            "AttributeName": "Username",
            "KeyType": "HASH"
          }
        ],
        "Projection": {
          "ProjectionType": "ALL"
        },
        "ProvisionedThroughput": {
          "ReadCapacityUnits": 1,
          "WriteCapacityUnits": 1
        }
      }
    ],
    "ProvisionedThroughput": {
      "ReadCapacityUnits": 1,
      "WriteCapacityUnits": 1
    }
  }
}
```

First of all, note that we added `Username` to the `AttributeDefinitions` section. It is needed for any attribute that is indexed because DynamoDB wants to know the type of the attribute upfront-String, in our case. After that, we define a GSI with the `Username` attribute as HASH, and we adjust `Projection` to ALL, which means that when we query the table using this index, it will return all the documents, and then we set the read and write provisioned throughput capacity. To understand better how indexes work, it is strongly recommended that you refer to the AWS documentation, but for our use case, this configuration is just sufficient. You might have asked why we defined the new provisioned throughput capacity. That is because global secondary indexes are just behaving as different tables, and they have their own read and write capacity. Of course, it creates an extra cost for every extra index, and you have to predict the potential usage of your indexes and set throughput capacities accordingly.

Before you create another index, you have to deploy your project. This is because of an interesting AWS limitation: At any one time, you can only add one global secondary index. If we add the second index now and try to deploy all the changes at one time, they would fail. That's why, you should deploy it now and wait until the process finishes.

The second index we need now is `EmailIndex`. It is almost the same as `UsernameIndex`, so as the attribute definition, we should add the following:

```
{
    "AttributeName": "Email",
    "AttributeType": "S"
}
```

Add this definition to Global Secondary Indexes:

```
{
    "IndexName": "EmailIndex",
    "KeySchema": [
      {
         "AttributeName": "Email",
         "KeyType": "HASH"
      }
    ],
    "Projection": {
       "ProjectionType": "ALL"
    },
    "ProvisionedThroughput": {
       "ReadCapacityUnits": 1,
       "WriteCapacityUnits": 1
    }
}
```

We should deploy to create the second index again.

We have our indexes ready, so now, we can move on to modifying our application. We will start with `UserRepository` first. Here, we need some methods, such as `getUserByEmail`, `getUserByUsername`, and `saveUser`. The first two methods will fetch users from DynamoDB using different criteria, and the last one will save a new user or update an existing one.

DynamoDB Mapper saves our day again because it supports querying by global secondary indexes. However, a new annotation comes into the scene because DynamoDB Mapper needs to know which attributes correspond to global secondary indexes. If you want, let's start with modifying our `User` class for these new indexes. The changes are not too big, so we only have to change our field definitions, such as the following:

```
public class User {
    . . . . . . .

    @DynamoDBIndexHashKey(globalSecondaryIndexName = "UsernameIndex",
        attributeName = "Username")
    private String username;

    @DynamoDBIndexHashKey(globalSecondaryIndexName = "EmailIndex",
        attributeName = "Email")
    private String email;
    . . . . .
}
```

Now we can create three new methods in our `UserRepository` interface:

```
public interface UserRepository {
    . . . . .
    Optional<User> getUserByEmail(String email);
    Optional<User> getUserByUsername(String username);
    void saveUser(User user);
}
```

Now we will implement these methods. Let's start with `saveUser`, which is a one-line method:

```
public class UserRepositoryDynamoDB implements UserRepository {
    . . . . . .
    @Override
    public void saveUser(User user) {
        dynamoDBMapper.save(user);
    }
}
```

Now we can implement the other ones. Querying by global secondary index is a bit different than the primary index, so we need to write a method that will get the index name and the criteria as the parameter and return the result. Now add this method to the `UserRepositoryDynamoDB` class:

```
public class UserRepositoryDynamoDB implements UserRepository {
  .....
  public Optional<User> getUserByCriteria(String indexName,
    User hashKeyValues) {
    DynamoDBQueryExpression<User> expression = new
      DynamoDBQueryExpression<User>()
    .withIndexName(indexName)
    .withConsistentRead(false)
    .withHashKeyValues(hashKeyValues)
    .withLimit(1);

    QueryResultPage<User> result = dynamoDBMapper.queryPage(User.class,
      expression);
    if (result.getCount() > 0) {
      return Optional.of(result.getResults().get(0));
    }
    return Optional.empty();
  }
}
```

Using this method, it is very easy to fetch users by username or email. Then, we can add these two methods to finish the implementation:

```
@Override
public Optional<User> getUserByEmail(String email) {
  return getUserByCriteria("EmailIndex", new User().setEmail(email));
}

@Override
public Optional<User> getUserByUsername(String username) {
  return getUserByCriteria("UsernameIndex", new
    User().setUsername(username));
}
```

It is convenient to add a test to verify that our repository works correctly. Now create the test folder with this command:

```
$ mkdir -p services-user/src/test/java/com/
  serverlessbook/services/user/repository
```

Then, create `UserRepositoryDynamoDBTest.java` with the following content:

```java
package com.serverlessbook.services.user.repository;

import com.amazonaws.services.dynamodbv2.AmazonDynamoDBClient;
import com.serverlessbook.repository.DynamoDBMapperWithCustomTableName;
import com.serverlessbook.services.user.domain.User;
import org.junit.Test;
import java.util.Optional;
import java.util.UUID;
import static org.junit.Assert.*;

public class UserRepositoryDynamoDBTest {
  private UserRepository getUserRepository() {
      return new UserRepositoryDynamoDB(new
DynamoDBMapperWithCustomTableName(
        new AmazonDynamoDBClient()));
  }

  @Test
  public void saveAndRetrieveUser() throws Exception {
      final String email = "test@test.com";
      final String password = "test-password";
      final String username = "test-username";
      final String id = UUID.randomUUID().toString();

      User newUser = new User()
       .setEmail(email)
       .setUsername(username)
       .setId(id);

      getUserRepository().saveUser(newUser);
      assertEquals(email, getUserRepository().getUserByEmail
        (email).orElseThrow(RuntimeException::new).getEmail());
      assertEquals(username, getUserRepository().getUserByUsername
        (username).orElseThrow(RuntimeException::new).getUsername());
  }
}
```

As you might have noted, this test creates a user with a specific information and then tries to fetch the same user from DynamoDB and tests the availability of the object after querying. This test should pass, so you are good to go. Our repository is working.

Now it is time to implement the business logic. First, let's create the exceptions to be thrown when a check fails. Let's start with creating the `com.serverlessbook.services.user.exception` package and create the `UserRegistrationException` class under it:

```
package com.serverlessbook.services.user.exception;

public abstract class UserRegistrationException extends Exception {
    private static final long serialVersionUID = -7628860081079461234L;
    protected UserRegistrationException(String message) {
        super(message);
    }
}
```

This is our base exception, which will be thrown by `UserService`. Now, we have to create child exceptions for every case. Let's start with `InvalidMailAddressException`:

```
package com.serverlessbook.services.user.exception;

public class InvalidMailAddressException extends
 UserRegistrationException {
  private static final long serialVersionUID = 4033382620357808779L;
  public InvalidMailAddressException() {
    super("This E-Mail address is not valid");
  }
}
```

Then let's add two more exceptions with Java-ish names, first for duplicate usernames:

```
package com.serverlessbook.services.user.exception;

public class AnotherUserWithSameUsernameExistsException extends
 UserRegistrationException {
    private static final long serialVersionUID = 4824390458386666422L;
    public AnotherUserWithSameUsernameExistsException() {
        super("Another user with same username already exists.");
    }
}
```

And then let's add duplicate email addresses:

```
package com.serverlessbook.services.user.exception;

public class AnotherUserWithSameEmailExistsException extends
UserRegistrationException {
    private static final long serialVersionUID = -7048567407775970663L;
    public AnotherUserWithSameEmailExistsException() {
      super("Another user with same E-Mail address already exists.");
    }
}
```

Now we add the required methods to `UserService`:

```
public interface UserService {
   ....
   User registerNewUser(String username, String email) throws
     UserRegistrationException;
}
```

You might ask why we do not expect a password at this stage, just like all modern web applications. In the next chapter, we will trigger another Lambda function whenever a new user is added to our system. This Lambda function will generate a password for the user and send it via email to the user. Why don't we do this in the `registerNewUser` function? There are two answers for this question. First, because of the separation of concerns principle. This method should be responsible only for creating the user and persisting it on the database. Whatever you want to do when a new user is registered to you is up to you. In our case, we will send an email, but we may want to do 10 more different things when a user is added. You should create 10 different functions in this case and trigger them via **SNS (Simple Notification System)**, which we will see in the next chapter.

There is also a practical benefit of such a approach. Sending emails or performing other post-registration processes takes time and the client does not have to wait for them to be completed. So, running them asynchronously will reduce the response time after registration and improve your response time.

Now we can implement the `registerNewUser` method:

```
@Override
public User registerNewUser(String username, String email) throws
  UserRegistrationException {
    checkEmailValidity(email);
    checkEmailUniqueness(email);
    checkUsernameUniqueness(username);

    User newUser = new User()
      .setId(UUID.randomUUID().toString())
      .setUsername(username)
      .setEmail(email);

    userRepository.saveUser(newUser);
    return newUser;
}
```

Here, we need three methods that will perform three different checks:

```
private void checkEmailValidity(String email) throws
  InvalidMailAddressException {
    final String emailPattern = "^[a-zA-Z0-9.!#$%&'*+/=?^_`{|}~-
]+@((\\[[0-9]{1,3}\\.
  [0-9]{1,3}\\.[0-9]{1,3}\\.[0-9]{1,3}\\])|(([a-zA-Z\\-0-9]+\\.)+[a-zA-
Z]{2,}))$";
    if (!Pattern.compile(emailPattern).matcher(email).matches()) {
      throw new InvalidMailAddressException();
    }
}

void checkEmailUniqueness(String email) throws
AnotherUserWithSameEmailExistsException {
  if (userRepository.getUserByEmail(email).isPresent()) {
      throw new AnotherUserWithSameEmailExistsException();
  }
}

void checkUsernameUniqueness(String username) throws
  AnotherUserWithSameUsernameExistsException {
    if (userRepository.getUserByUsername(username).isPresent()) {
      throw new AnotherUserWithSameUsernameExistsException();
    }
}
```

These methods just throw the appropriate extensions when the check fails. Now we can create a test for this class and make sure that it works before we upload it to Lambda. Let's create the skeleton for the test first:

```
package com.serverlessbook.services.user;

import com.amazonaws.services.dynamodbv2.AmazonDynamoDBClient;
import com.serverlessbook.repository.DynamoDBMapperWithCustomTableName;
import com.serverlessbook.services.user.repository.UserRepositoryDynamoDB;
import org.junit.Rule;
import org.junit.rules.ExpectedException;

public class UserServiceImplTest {
  @Rule
  public ExpectedException thrown = ExpectedException.none();
  private UserService getUserService() {
    return new UserServiceImpl(new UserRepositoryDynamoDB(new
      DynamoDBMapperWithCustomTableName(new AmazonDynamoDBClient())));
  }
}
```

Now we can create three different tests for three different failing cases:

```
@Test
public void failedUserRegistrationWithExistingUsernameTest() throws
Exception {
    thrown.expect(AnotherUserWithSameUsernameExistsException.class);
    UserService userService = getUserService();
    final String username = UUID.randomUUID() + "test-username";
    userService.registerNewUser(username, UUID.randomUUID() + "@test.com");
    //Second call should fail
    userService.registerNewUser(username, UUID.randomUUID() + "@test.com");
}
```

The second one is for the existing email addresses:

```
@Test
public void failedUserRegistrationWithExistingEMailTest() throws Exception
{
    thrown.expect(AnotherUserWithSameEmailExistsException.class);
    UserService userService = getUserService();
    final String email = UUID.randomUUID() + "@test.com";
    userService.registerNewUser(UUID.randomUUID().toString(), email);
    //Second call should fail
    userService.registerNewUser(UUID.randomUUID().toString(), email);
}
```

And finally, we have one for invalid emails:

```
@Test
public void failedUserRegistrationWithInvalidEmailTest() throws Exception {
    thrown.expect(InvalidMailAddressException.class);
    UserService userService = getUserService();
    userService.registerNewUser(UUID.randomUUID().toString(),
    "INVALID_EMAIL");
}
```

And we are good with tests.

 Actually, any seasoned engineer can note that our testing approach has some flaws. These are not unit tests because they use a real implementation of dependent objects or because we are testing against a live database, and so on. All of the criticism is correct; this is not how you test your software. However, the scope of this book is not to teach Java or basic software engineering principles, but the peculiarities of the AWS ecosystem. Therefore, we will keep our tests like this. In your production system, you should consider developing a better structured test approach.

Creating user registration Lambda

It is now time to create our second real Lambda function: User Registration Lambda. Create the required directory structure and add the lambda-userregistration module to the settings.gradle file so that Gradle accepts it as a module:

```
$ mkdir -p lambda-userregistration/src/main/java/
  com/serverlessbook/lambda/userregistration
$ echo "include 'lambda-userregistration " >> settings.gradle
```

We have to create a build.gradle file for this module and dependencies for the user service and Guice, which is pretty much the same as the authorizer Lambda. Let's create the file first:

```
$ touch lambda-userregistration/build.gradle
```

Then, let's paste this block:

```
dependencies {
    compile group: 'com.google.inject', name: 'guice', version:
guiceVersion
    compile project(':services-user')
}
```

Now we can create the handler class:

```
public class Handler extends LambdaHandler<Handler.RegistrationInput,
  Handler.RegistrationOutput> {
  public static class RegistrationInput {
    @JsonProperty("username")
    private String username;
    @JsonProperty("email")
    private String email;

    public String getUsername() {
      return username;
    }

    public String getEmail() {
      return email;
    }
  }
  public static class RegistrationOutput {
    private final String resourceUrl;
    public RegistrationOutput(User user) {
      resourceUrl = "/user/" + user.getId();
    }

    @JsonGetter("resourceUrl")
    public String getResourceUrl() {
      return resourceUrl;
    }
  }
  @Override public RegistrationOutput handleRequest(RegistrationInput
input,
    Context context) {
    return null;
  }
}
```

For the sake of simplicity, this time, we used static inner classes for input and output instead of creating different files for these classes. For input, we will accept a JSON with email and username properties, and for output, we will return only the resource URL of the generated user.

As per REST conventions, a POST request should return with 201 HTTP code with an empty body and the URL of the newly created resource in the Location header. On the API Gateway layer, we will use the output value to construct the Location header. Indeed, we won't be creating the endpoint for the user in this book; that is up to you.

We should add the dependency injection part to the handler as well, just like the the authorizer Lambda:

```
public class Handler extends LambdaHandler<Handler.RegistrationInput,
Handler.RegistrationOutput> {
  .....
  private static final Injector INJECTOR = Guice.createInjector(new
    DependencyInjectionModule());

  private UserService userService;

  @Inject
  public void setUserService(UserService userService) {
    this.userService = userService;
  }

  public Handler() {
    INJECTOR.injectMembers(this);
    Objects.requireNonNull(userService);
  }
  ...
}
```

We should create `DependencyInjectionModule` for this new Lambda again, with almost the same content as the authorizer Lambda. Let's create the file:

```
$ touch lambda-userregistration/src/main/java/com/serverlessbook/
  lambda/userregistration/DependencyInjectionModule.java
```

Then let's use the following code:

```
package com.serverlessbook.lambda.userregistration;

import com.amazonaws.services.dynamodbv2.datamodeling.DynamoDBMapper;
import com.google.inject.AbstractModule;
import com.serverlessbook.repository.DynamoDBMapperWithCustomTableName;
import com.serverlessbook.services.user.UserService;
import com.serverlessbook.services.user.UserServiceImpl;
import com.serverlessbook.services.user.repository.UserRepository;
import com.serverlessbook.services.user.repository.UserRepositoryDynamoDB;
```

```
public class DependencyInjectionModule extends AbstractModule {
  @Override
  protected void configure() {
     bind(UserService.class).to(UserServiceImpl.class);
     bind(UserRepository.class).to(UserRepositoryDynamoDB.class);
bind(DynamoDBMapper.class).to(DynamoDBMapperWithCustomTableName.class);
  }
}
```

Now we can implement our handle method in the Handler class:

```
@Override
public RegistrationOutput handleRequest(RegistrationInput input, Context
context) {
   User createdUser = userService.registerNewUser(input.username,
input.email);
   return new RegistrationOutput(createdUser);
}
```

Did you notice an issue here? Our compiler complains because `registerNewUser` is throwing an exception. However, we do not want to catch this exception as any uncaught exception will cause Lambda to fail, and consequently, we can handle this error to produce HTTP error code in API Gateway. As you may know, any checked exception deriving from `Exception` should be caught or reported in the method signature, as is also the case with our `UserRegistrationException` exceptions. But if an exception derived from `RuntimeException` does not have this limitation, then we can solve this issue by changing `UserRegistrationException` with the following style:

```
public abstract class UserRegistrationException extends RuntimeException {
   private static final long serialVersionUID = -7628860081079461234L;

   protected UserRegistrationException(String message) {
      super(message);
   }
}
```

Creating the Lambda and API Gateway for User Registration

After we create our code for user registration, it is time to create a Lambda function and configure it to use with API Gateway. As a first step, let's create a new Lambda function in our CloudFormation template:

```json
"UserRegistrationLambda": {
  "Type": "AWS::Lambda::Function",
  "Properties": {
    "Handler": "com.serverlessbook.lambda.userregistration.Handler",
    "Runtime": "java8",
    "Timeout": "300",
    "MemorySize": "1024",
    "Description": "User registration Lambda",
    "Role": {
      "Fn::GetAtt": [
        "LambdaExecutionRole",
        "Arn"
      ]
    },
    "Code": {
     "S3Bucket": {
       "Ref": "DeploymentBucket"
      },
      "S3Key": {
        "Fn::Sub": "artifacts/lambda-
            userregistration/${ProjectVersion}/${DeploymentTime}.jar"
      }
    },
    "Environment": {
      "Variables": {
        "DynamoDbTokenTable": {
          "Ref": "TokenTable"
         },
         "DynamoDbUserTable": {
           "Ref": "UserTable"
          }
        }
      }
    }
  }
}
```

This is pretty much the same code as other Lambda functions, except the S3Key property.

The second step will be to create the REST resource. We will create a resource with the /user path:

```json
"UsersResource": {
  "Type": "AWS::ApiGateway::Resource",
  "Properties": {
    "PathPart": "users",
    "RestApiId": {
        "Ref": "RestApi"
      },
```

```
            "ParentId": {
               "Fn::GetAtt": [
                   "RestApi",
                   "RootResourceId"
               ]
            }
         }
     }
 }
```

This part was also very similar to the other resource we created previously. We just changed `PathPart` with `users`, which will create an `http://domain.com/users` URL.

The most important part is the configuration of the method. Let's add this block to our template now:

```
"UsersPostMethod": {
    "Type": "AWS::ApiGateway::Method",
    "Properties": {
      "HttpMethod": "POST",
      "RestApiId": {
         "Ref": "RestApi"
      },
      "ResourceId": {
         "Ref": "UsersResource"
      },
      "AuthorizationType": "NONE",
        "RequestParameters": {
      },
      "MethodResponses": [
        {
           "StatusCode": "201",
           "ResponseParameters": {
               "method.response.header.Location": "true"
           }
        },
        {
           "StatusCode": "400"
        },
        {
           "StatusCode": "409"
        }
      ],
      "Integration": {
        "Type": "AWS",
        "Uri": {
           "Fn::Sub": "arn:aws:apigateway:${AWS::Region}:lambda:path/
           2015-03-31/functions/${UserRegistrationLambda.Arn}/invocations"
        },
```

```
      "IntegrationHttpMethod": "POST",
      "RequestParameters": {
      },
      "RequestTemplates": {
        "application/json": "{\"username\": $input.json('$.username'),
         \"email\": $input.json('$.email')}"
      },
      "PassthroughBehavior": "NEVER",
        "IntegrationResponses": [
          {
            "SelectionPattern": ".*",
            "StatusCode": "201",
            "ResponseParameters": {
            "method.response.header.Location":
"integration.response.body.resourceUrl"
          },
            "ResponseTemplates": {
            "application/json": "#set($inputRoot = $input.path('$'))"
          }
        },
        {
          "SelectionPattern": ".*not valid.*",
          "StatusCode": "400",
          "ResponseTemplates": {
            "application/json": "{\"code\": 400,
             \"errorMessage\":\"$input.path('$.errorMessage')\"}"
          }
        },
        {
          "SelectionPattern": ".*already exists.*",
          "StatusCode": "409",
          "ResponseTemplates": {
            "application/json": "{\"code\": 409,
             \"errorMessage\":\"$input.path('$.errorMessage')\"}"
          }
        }
      ]
    }
  }
}
```

In the following sections, we will look at what we do here in more detail, so do not worry if it seems complicated. Briefly, we use regular expressions to alter HTTP status code when there is an error. When the method is successful, we tell API Gateway to return an empty response and also set the `Location` header with the `resourceUrl` property of our output.

We should not forget to create a `AWS::Lambda::Permission` resource in order to allow API Gateway to execute Lambda on our behalf:

```
"UsersPostLambdaPermission": {
  "Type": "AWS::Lambda::Permission",
  "Properties": {
    "Action": "lambda:InvokeFunction",
    "FunctionName": {
      "Ref": "UserRegistrationLambda"
    },
    "Principal": "apigateway.amazonaws.com",
      "SourceArn": {
      "Fn::Sub": "arn:aws:execute-api:${AWS::Region}:
        ${AWS::AccountId}:${RestApi}/*"
    }
  }
}
```

We are now ready to test our API with different scenarios.

Let's try with an invalid email address first:

```
$ curl -X POST  -H "Content-Type: application/json" -d
 '{"username": "testuser", email:  "invalidemail"}'
 https://serverlessbook.merkurapp.com/users
 {"code": 400, "errorMessage":"This E-Mail address is not valid"}
```

It returned an HTTP 400 error:

```
$ curl  -X POST  -H "Content-Type: application/json" -d
 '{"username": "tester2", email: "test@tester.com"}' -v
 https://serverlessbook.merkurapp.com/users
```

This will return a 201 HTTP code and also a Location header in which we can access that user if we implement it.

Trying the same request for a second time will fail because there is already a user with the same information.

Try this with duplicate mail addresses and usernames and see whether the API fails.

Summary

This chapter was an important step because we implemented a very good structured application with the dependency injection pattern and created an API endpoint using that. We looked at how to persist our data without having a database system that needs maintenance. Adding more tables and consuming them with more endpoints like these is up to you and your business requirements. You will need the help of the AWS documentation to discover more features of DynamoDB and API Gateway that can be useful for you.

In the next chapter, we will switch our focus a bit more to other AWS parts, such as **SNS (Simple Notification Service)**, **SES (Simple E-Mail Service)**, and S3. First, we will notify an asynchronous Lambda that will set the password for our newly registered users and send a welcome mail to them along with it. In the second part, we will work on an even more exciting topic: our users will upload their profile pictures to S3 buckets with the permission we give, and using 0 custom code, we will resize those photos asynchronously and save them back in the S3 bucket.

6

Building Supporting Services

In the previous chapter, we saw how we can invoke Lambda functions when a client requests an HTTP source. It was not so different from a classical web application, and instead of a controller class always in memory, Lambda runtime located our code piece to execute it and removed it from memory after it finished its job. We only paid for what we used, and we did not have to maintain any infrastructure on our own.

Is it the only way to benefit from Lambdas? Definitely not.

Let's assume that our forum application got very popular and we wanted to let our users upload their profile pictures. In different parts of our forum, we will be using three different sizes of profile pictures, so whenever a user uploads a new picture, we should resize the image on a data storage. The first thing that comes to mind is to create another Lambda function to respond to the HTTP upload request and to resize images on the fly, but we can never guarantee that our resize process will last a reasonable amount of time. Also, with this architecture, we are again binding the HTTP context with our business context; it means our Lambda function will have to deal with two different contexts.

AWS brings a better solution to this problem. With API Gateway, we can expose a limited functionality of our cloud resources to end user, and we can trigger Lambda functions when some specific events occur in the cloud resources. In this chapter, we will build an asynchronous image-resizing service, and the only piece of code we will write will be to resize the image. In this chapter, we will cover the following topics:

- How to configure API Gateway to let users upload their files to S3 without code
- How to trigger Lambda functions when a new file is added to the S3 bucket
- How to configure CloudFront to serve files directly through the S3 bucket

Writing the foundation of a Lambda function

We can start our task with writing a Lambda function, which responds to S3 events and will resize the image. At this stage, the code will not resize the image, but it will only log the request, so first, we can see that the function is really triggered by S3.

As usual, we can create our new module with the name `lambda-imageresizer`:

```
$ mkdir -p lambda-imageresize/src/main/java/com/
    serverlessbook/lambda/imageresize
```

Then, let's add this new module to our `settings.gradle` file:

```
$ echo "include 'lambda-imageresizer'" >> settings.gradle
```

We can now create our `Handler` class in the `com.serverlessbook.lambda.imageresize` package:

```
$ touch lambda-imageresizer/src/main/java/com/serverlessbook/lambda/
    imageresizer/Handler.java
```

In this Lambda function, we will consume standardized events prepared by S3. AWS provides a Java package that includes POJOs for this type of event, including S3. This package can be found in the Maven repository by the name `com.amazonaws:aws-lambda-java-events`. It means our job is even easier now, because we neither have to create a model for the incoming event nor use our own JSON deserialization procedures. Then, we will first create a `build.gradle` method in the `lambda-imageresizer` module and add the necessary dependency:

```
dependencies {
    compile group: 'com.amazonaws', name: 'aws-lambda-java-events',
      version: '1.3.0'
}
```

We create the preliminary version of our `Handler` method as follows:

```java
package com.serverlessbook.lambda.imageresizer;

import com.amazonaws.services.lambda.runtime.Context;
import com.amazonaws.services.lambda.runtime.RequestHandler;
import com.amazonaws.services.lambda.runtime.events.S3Event;
import org.apache.log4j.Logger;

public class Handler implements RequestHandler<S3Event, Void> {

  private static final Logger LOGGER = Logger.getLogger(Handler.class);

  private void resizeImage(String bucket, String key) {
    LOGGER.info("Resizing s3://" + bucket + "/" + key);
  }

  @Override
  public Void handleRequest(S3Event input, Context context) {
    input.getRecords().forEach(s3EventNotificationRecord ->
      resizeImage(s3EventNotificationRecord.getS3().getBucket().getName(),
      s3EventNotificationRecord.getS3().getObject().getKey()));
    return null;
  }
}
```

As you have seen, the built-in library of AWS made it very easy, and we have already access to the most important information of the newly added file to the S3 bucket. When a new file is added to the bucket by any means, this Lambda function will be invoked and the `resizeImage` function will execute. In this function, we will resize the image and save it to the same bucket with a user ID. We will see in detail how we will get the user ID from the file saved at S3.

Now, let's create a Lambda function using this artifact. Let's add a new resource to `cloudformation.json`:

```json
"ImageResizerLambda": {
  "Type": "AWS::Lambda::Function",
  "Properties": {
    "Handler": "com.serverlessbook.lambda.imageresizer.Handler",
    "Runtime": "java8",
    "Timeout": "300",
    "MemorySize": "1024",
    "Description": "Test lambda",
    "Role": {
      "Fn::GetAtt": [
        "LambdaExecutionRole",
```

```
            "Arn"
        ]
    },
    "Code": {
      "S3Bucket": {
        "Ref": "DeploymentBucket"
      },
      "S3Key": {
        "Fn::Sub": "artifacts/lambda-imageresizer/${ProjectVersion}/
            ${DeploymentTime}.jar"
      }
    }
  }
}
```

Let's now create the S3 bucket:

```
"ProfilePicturesBucket": {
  "Type": "AWS::S3::Bucket",
  "Properties": {
    "BucketName": {
      "Fn::Sub": "${DomainName}-profilepictures"
    }
  }
}
```

 As you noted, the S3 bucket will be created using the `DomainName` value you gave in the main `build.gradle` file. Be careful about using a unique domain name, as any other reader of the book might be using the same domain name, and there can be only one S3 bucket with the same name on all AWS.

We can now add the event configuration to the S3 bucket. Let's just add the following snippet under the `BucketName` property as a new property:

```
"NotificationConfiguration": {
  "LambdaConfigurations": [
    {
      "Event": "s3:ObjectCreated:*",
      "Filter": {
        "S3Key": {
          "Rules": [
            {
              "Name": "prefix",
              "Value": "uploads/"
            }
          ]
```

```
      }
    },
    "Function": {
      "Fn::GetAtt": [
        "ImageResizerLambda",
        "Arn"
      ]
    }
  }
]
}
```

Here, note the `Event` and `Filter` values. Setting the Event value to `s3:ObjectCreated:*` tells AWS that our Lambda function should only be called when a new object is added to the bucket. We could also call Lambda when an object is deleted, but it is not our case for now. The `Filter` value is limiting the invocation of the Lambda. Our Lambda will be called only in the `uploads/` folder, because our users will be uploading their profile pictures to that folder. It is important to use filters because once our Lambda function executes, it will save the resized photos to another folder. If we had not limited this event, our Lambda function would also cause another execution of itself, such as a recursive function, and it would be an endless loop.

At this stage, we configured the event, but S3 is still not permitted to invoke our Lambda. Remember that in the previous chapter, we created an authorizer at the API Gateway layer, and we created an `AWS::Lambda::Permission` resource to let the `apigateway.amazonaws.com` principal to execute our function. Here, we will do something very similar. Let's add this snippet to our resources:

```
"ImageResizerLambdaPermisson": {
  "Type": "AWS::Lambda::Permission",
    "Properties": {
      "Action": "lambda:InvokeFunction",
      "FunctionName": {
        "Ref": "ImageResizerLambda"
      },
      "Principal": "s3.amazonaws.com",
      "SourceArn": {
        "Fn::Sub": "arn:aws:s3:::${DomainName}-profilepictures"
      }
    }
}
```

Now, our Lambda can be executed by S3 on our behalf.

At this stage, you can try to upload a file to the bucket, but to the uploads/ folder, and see that the Lambda function is automatically executed and writes a log entry to CloudWatch.

Letting users upload to S3

As the second part of this picture-resizing system, we need to create an endpoint that will let our users upload their pictures to the S3 bucket. As we explained at the beginning, there is no need to develop any custom software for that because API Gateway, besides executing Lambda functions, also lets us expose some of AWS APIs to public the internet. It means, we can let API Gateway clients use the S3 upload API on our behalf.

How can we configure this? First, we have to create a new role that can be assumed by API Gateway and only grants s3:PutObject and s3:PutObjectAcl permissions to our profile pictures bucket. Let's add this permission to our Resources section of the CloudFormation template:

```
"ApiGatewayProxyRole": {
  "Type": "AWS::IAM::Role",
    "Properties": {
      "AssumeRolePolicyDocument": {
        "Version": "2012-10-17",
        "Statement": [
          {
            "Effect": "Allow",
            "Principal": {
             "Service": [
               "apigateway.amazonaws.com"
               ]
            },
            "Action": "sts:AssumeRole"
          }
        ]
      },
      "Path": "/",
      "Policies": [
        {
          "PolicyName": "S3BucketPolicy",
          "PolicyDocument": {
            "Version": "2012-10-17",
            "Statement": [
              {
                "Effect": "Allow",
                "Action": [
                  "s3:PutObject",
```

```
                "s3:PutObjectAcl"
            ],
            "Resource": [
                {
                    "Fn::Sub": "arn:aws:s3:::${ProfilePicturesBucket}"
                },
                {
                    "Fn::Sub": "arn:aws:s3:::${ProfilePicturesBucket}/*"
                }
            ]
        }
    ]
}
}
]
}
}
```

Now, we can create REST resources for the endpoint. We will put our method to the `/users/{userid}/picture` path, and we will create a PUT method for updating the profile picture:

```
"UsersIdResource": {
  "Type": "AWS::ApiGateway::Resource",
    "Properties": {
    "PathPart": "{id}",
    "RestApiId": {
      "Ref": "RestApi"
    },
    "ParentId": {
      "Ref": "UsersResource"
    }
  }
},
"UsersIdPictureResource": {
  "Type": "AWS::ApiGateway::Resource",
    "Properties": {
      "PathPart": "picture",
      "RestApiId": {
        "Ref": "RestApi"
      },
      "ParentId": {
        "Ref": "UsersIdResource"
      }
    }
}
```

Now, we can add the PUT method to the proxy S3 call:

```
"UsersIdPicturePutMethod": {
  "Type": "AWS::ApiGateway::Method",
    "Properties": {
      "HttpMethod": "PUT",
      "RestApiId": {
        "Ref": "RestApi"
      },
      "AuthorizationType": "CUSTOM",
       "AuthorizerId": {
         "Ref": "ApiGatewayAuthorizer"
       },
       "ResourceId": {
         "Ref": "UsersIdPictureResource"
       },
       "RequestParameters": {
         "method.request.path.id": "True",
         "method.request.header.Content-Type": "True",
         "method.request.header.Content-Length": "True"
       },
       "Integration": {
         "Type": "AWS",
         "Uri": {
           "Fn::Sub": "arn:aws:apigateway:${AWS::Region}:s3:path/
             ${ProfilePicturesBucket}/uploads/{filename}"
         },
         "IntegrationHttpMethod": "PUT",
         "Credentials": {
           "Fn::GetAtt": [
             "ApiGatewayProxyRole",
             "Arn"
           ]
         },
         "RequestParameters": {
           "integration.request.path.filename": "context.requestId",
           "integration.request.header.Content-Type":
           "method.request.header.Content-Type",
           "integration.request.header.Content-Length":
           "method.request.header.Content-Length",
           "integration.request.header.Expect": "'100-continue'",
           "integration.request.header.x-amz-acl": "'public-read'",
           "integration.request.header.x-amz-meta-user-id":
"method.request.path.id"
         },
         "RequestTemplates": {
         },
         "PassthroughBehavior": "WHEN_NO_TEMPLATES",
```

```json
        "IntegrationResponses": [
          {
            "SelectionPattern": "4\\d{2}",
            "StatusCode": "400"
          },
          {
            "SelectionPattern": "5\\d{2}",
            "StatusCode": "500"
          },
          {
            "SelectionPattern": ".*",
            "StatusCode": "202",
            "ResponseTemplates": {
              "application/json": {
                "Fn::Sub": "{\"status\": \"pending\"}"
              }
            }
          }
        ]
      },
      "MethodResponses": [
        {
          "StatusCode": "202"
        },
        {
          "StatusCode": "400"
        },
        {
          "StatusCode": "500"
        }
      ]
    }
  }
```

This method definition may seem a bit complicated. What we are doing here is mapping HTTP request properties coming from API Gateway to the S3 API calls. We are passing through the request body to S3 API, and in the case of a successful call, we are returning 202 Accepted response. The reason for using this status code is that our image processing is asynchronous; therefore, we have to signal the client that its request has been accepted and currently is being processed. Note that we are using the automatically generated API Gateway request ID to generate the uploaded file's name (`integration.request.path.filename": "context.requestId`). The uploaded file will be saved in the `upload/` folder and with this random name. But how will our Lambda function tell the user ID of the uploaded picture? We will use S3's file metadata feature for this (`integration.request.header.x-amz-meta-user-id":` `"method.request.path.id"`). We are reading the `id` value from the request path and passing it to the S3 API. S3 then saves the `user-id` metadata to the uploaded photo, which can be read by the Lambda function.

We enabled the Lambda authorizer for this method, which means this method can be only called with an authorization token. However, as you might have noted, in this case, every authenticated user can modify the profile picture of someone else. In the following sections, we will modify our authorizer to prevent this situation.

After uploading the stack, you can try to upload an image to S3 using the API Gateway endpoint. You can use the following command, adapting it to your domain and a local image:

```
$ curl --data-binary @${HOME} /test.jpg  -X PUT -H
  "Content-Type: image/jpeg" -H "Authorization: Bearer validtoken"
  https://example.com/users/1234-1234-1234-1234/picture
```

You can see the uploaded image on the S3 bucket. Use this command to replace the bucket:

```
$ aws s3 ls YOUR_DOMAIN-profilepictures/uploads/
```

If you browse the S3 bucket and try to download the image, you can see that the image data is invalid. It is because the uploaded file has been treated as UTF-8 text. To tell API Gateway to treat specific `Content-Type` headers as a binary, we have to manually configure it. You can do it by navigating to API Gateway console, opening your API, clicking on **Binary Support**, and adding the desired content types. Here, we added `image/png` and `image/jpeg` as binary types, but you can add more according to your needs:

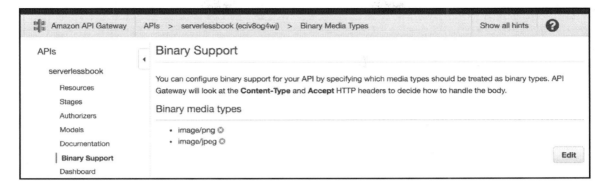

Unfortunately, this operation is not supported via CloudFormation; therefore, we have to do it manually.

Modifying the Lambda function to respond to an S3 event

Now, we have to modify our Lambda function to respond to an S3 event. As it is beyond the scope of our book, we will not implement any resizing logic at the moment. We will only copy the uploaded picture to the appropriate directory. Now, let's modify our Handler class in the `lambda-imageresizer` module:

```
public class Handler implements RequestHandler<S3Event, Void> {
  private static final Logger LOGGER = Logger.getLogger(Handler.class);
  final AmazonS3 s3client;
  public Handler() {
    s3client = new AmazonS3Client(new
      DefaultAWSCredentialsProviderChain());
  }
  private void resizeImage(String bucket, String key) {
    LOGGER.info("Resizing s3://" + bucket + "/" + key);
    final String userId = s3client.getObjectMetadata(bucket,
      key).getUserMetaDataOf("user-id");
    LOGGER.info("Image is belonging to " + userId);
    final String destinationKey = "users/" + userId + "/picture/small.jpg";
    s3client.copyObject(bucket, key,
      bucket, destinationKey);
    LOGGER.info("Image has been copied to s3://" + bucket + "/"
      + destinationKey);
  }
  ...
}
```

Here, we created an S3 client in the constructor. In the `resizeImage` method, we read the metadata of the object that we set on the API Gateway layer. This metadata value is our user ID, and we constructed the destination path (`users/USER_ID/picture/small.jpg`) using this value. To really resize the image, you can use a couple of libraries available in the Java ecosystem.

> At this point, it is convenient to mention about a feature of Lambda functions. Note that we created the S3 client object inside the constructor. If you've put a log line inside the constructor and called the Lambda function more than one time, you would see that this log line is not called per every request. The reason for this behavior is hidden behind how Lambda runtime works. Whenever there is a new request to Lambda, AWS searches for an instance of this function globally on a machine. If an instance is not found, a new instance is created, the handler method is called, and the instance is left on the memory for the next request. There is approximately a 20 minutes' window until an unused Lambda function is totally destroyed from memory. However, for the subsequent requests, the same instance of Lambda is repeatedly used. If you have a reusable object whose creation is expensive, you can put it outside of the handler method to cache it among different requests. Due to the serverless nature, you cannot be sure that this object is cached among requests, but in practice, it generally is. This is an undocumented feature of Lambda and very useful to know for better performance.

Configuring CloudFront to serve resized images

The next step is to configure the CloudFront distribution to serve images directly from the S3 bucket. By this way, again with zero code, we will expose the S3 bucket to the public internet transparently.

CloudFront supports different configurations for different paths. It means you can forward specific requests to another origin if the request path is configured to do that. At the moment, our CloudFront is configured to forward all requests to API Gateway and now we will add another configuration to forward the requests coming to the `/users/USER_ID/picture/*` path to the S3 Bucket.

We can start with adding a new origin to our CloudFront distribution. Let's add this origin to the `CloudformationDistribution.Properties.Origins` section:

```
{
  "DomainName": {
    "Fn::Sub": "${ProfilePicturesBucket}.s3.amazonaws.com"
  },
  "Id": "PROFILE_PICTURES",
  "S3OriginConfig ": {
  }
}
```

Adding an S3 bucket as an origin is pretty straightforward. We just added `s3.amazonaws.com` to the bucket's name, and that's it.

Now, we have to configure a new cache behavior. Let's add this block just under the `DefaultCacheBehavior` section of the CloudFront distribution:

```
"CacheBehaviors": [
  {
    "PathPattern": "/users/*/picture/*",
    "TargetOriginId": "PROFILE_PICTURES",
    "Compress": true,
    "AllowedMethods": [
      "GET",
      "HEAD",
      "OPTIONS"
    ],
    "ForwardedValues": {
      "QueryString": "false",
      "Cookies": {
        "Forward": "none"
      }
    },
    "DefaultTTL": 0,
    "MinTTL": 0,
    "MaxTTL": 0,
    "ViewerProtocolPolicy": "redirect-to-https"
  }
]
```

You can add as many cache behaviors as you want. Here, we disabled HTTP caching, setting all cache TTLs to 0 because we want CloudFront to check S3 for every request for a new profile picture.

A different approach would be to create a random URL for every new profile picture. In that case, we could cache profile pictures using CloudFront. However, with this approach, we would need to create a new endpoint to get the latest profile picture URL for each user. It is up to you to choose the approach! Why not to try implement a solution like that?

Now, deploy the stack. Very likely, Gradle will timeout because as you experienced before, CloudFront updates take time because AWS has to propagate all your changes globally. You can monitor CloudFormation progress on the AWS console.

Once the deployment finishes, you can open your browser and navigate to `https://YOURDOMAIN/users/1234-1234-1234-1234/picture/small.jpg`. You will see that your uploaded image is now there.

Excercise

As we mentioned earlier, now, the API Gateway authorizes every valid token, and users can change each other's profile pictures. How would you prevent it and make sure that one can only change their own profile picture?

 Unfortunately, due to lack of features of API Gateway, you can't prevent people from uploading pictures on behalf of other users. However, you can save the uploader user ID as a new metadata to an S3 object. Then, you can modify your Lambda function to check the uploader user ID and the user ID whose profile picture is being updated. You can resize the image only when two values match.

You can pass the authorized user ID by adding a new request parameter on the method as follows:

```
"integration.request.header.x-amz-meta-uploader-user-id":
  "context.authorizer.principalId"
```

Sending emails via SES

One of the most used functionalities of a web application is to send emails to visitors. In our application, as you remember, we did not require the users to set a password, but we wanted to send a confirmation mail to their inboxes with an automatically generated password. AWS provides a great service for sending transactional emails, **SES (Simple E-Mail Service)** for this purpose. We can verify our domain in SES, set some DNS values for anti-spam purposes, and use the SES API to easily generate and send emails to our visitors.

In this section, we will briefly show you how to enable SES for sending emails. Moreover, we will introduce **SNS (Simple Notification Service)**, which is a messaging service in the cloud. In our architecture, our user registration Lambda will fire an SNS message to a topic, and we will have another Lambda that listens to this topic and sends an email to the newly registered user.

Could we not just add another line of code in our registration code to invoke the SES API so that we could send the email directly from that Lambda? Yes, we could, but in that case, we would have a tightly coupled system. The user registration Lambda is only responsible for registering the user to our database; the additional functionality that we may execute asynchronously should be implemented in additional functions, and we should trigger them via a messaging system. Maybe, in our application, we have only one operation that should be executed after the user registration, but in more complex systems, it is not unusual to see tens of different operations. In this case, it is a good idea to separate concerns and go to this type of architecture.

Configuring SES

To be able to use SES, we need to first configure our domain. It is possible to do so via a CLI client, but we will just use the AWS Console this time.

You can navigate to `https://console.aws.amazon.com/ses/` and click on the **Domains** links on the left pane. Here, you will see a **Verify New Domain** button:

After you click on the button, a new screen will appear, and you can write the domain you have been using throughout the book:

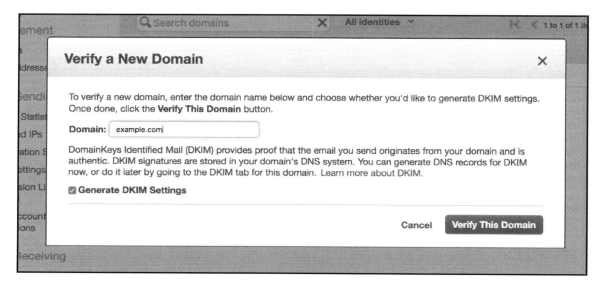

Do not forget to select the **Generate DKIM Settings** checkbox at this stage. DKIM is an email authentication method designed to detect email spoofing, and it is always a good idea to add these settings to our domain to ensure deliverability of our mails.

After clicking on the **Verify This Domain** button, some DNS records will be shown to be added to our domain's DNS records. Normally, you would have to add these records manually, but fortunately, we created a Route53 zone for our domain. So, the AWS Console will offer you the option to add these records to Route53 automatically. You can click on the **Use Route53** button to create the required records.

After creating the records, SES will automatically check the records and verify your domain automatically; however, this process may take some time.

Also, initially, your account will be in the sandbox mode that limits your sending abilities, and you have to open a support ticket to unlock your account. In order to accomplish this, you can navigate to `https://aws.amazon.com/ses/extendedaccessrequest/`and fill in the form.

Fortunately, SES provides a simulator that you can send mails to in the testing mode. Until you are out of the sandbox, you can use the simulator for testing purposes. Mails sent to `success@simulator.amazonses.com` will be always trigger a delivery event, while `bounce@simulator.amazonses.com` will result in a hard bounce. In the default configuration, bounced mails will be notified to you via your AWS account's mail, but in a production environment, you should configure SNS topics for unsuccessful sendings and evaluate this event to remove this recipient from your mail list or notify the mail's owner by other means that their mail address is not available any more.

Firing an SNS notification upon user registration

As we mentioned earlier, SNS is a very fundamental part of AWS that lets different parts of our software interact between each other via message passing. In SNS, you create topics and subscribe resources to them. Subscribers can be HTTP endpoints, Lambda functions, a mobile application, or you can even send SMS messages via SNS.

In this step, we will create an SNS topic for our user registration event and fire an event to that topic.

Let's start with adding our topic via the CloudFormation template. Add the following block to our `Resources` section:

```
"UserRegistrationSnsTopic": {
  "Type": "AWS::SNS::Topic",
  "Properties": {
    "Subscription": []
  }
}
```

After deploying your application, you can navigate to `https://console.aws.amazon.com/sns/v2/#/topics` to see the created topic.

Before going further, let's try SNS in action. As we mentioned earlier, you can subscribe an HTTP endpoint to SNS. Let's use `http://requestb.in/` to create a free HTTP POST bin that can show us any request coming to it. After entering the RequestBin website, click on the **Create a** RequestBin button to create a new request bin. In the next page, the URL for your sandbox will be shown. Copy it and go back to the SNS console. After selecting the topic, click on the **Actions** and **Subscribe to topic** buttons subsequently. Pick HTTP as the protocol and paste your RequestBin URL:

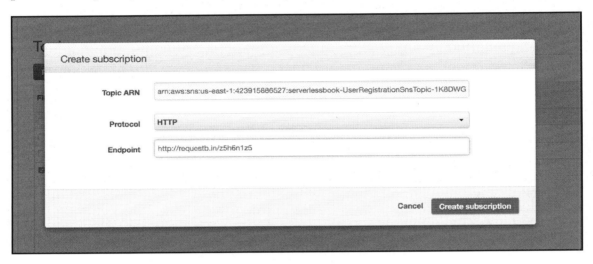

Now, go back to RequestBin, and you will see that SNS sent a POST message there. It is to confirm the subscription, and the **SubscribeURL** field in the incoming JSON will catch your attention. Copy this URL and paste to your browser to confirm the subscription. Now, your topic is subscribed by this fake HTTP endpoint, and you will see any message posted to this topic.

Now, back on the console, you can select your topic again and click on the **Publish to Topic** button. You can write any message in the text field and click on the **Publish message** button:

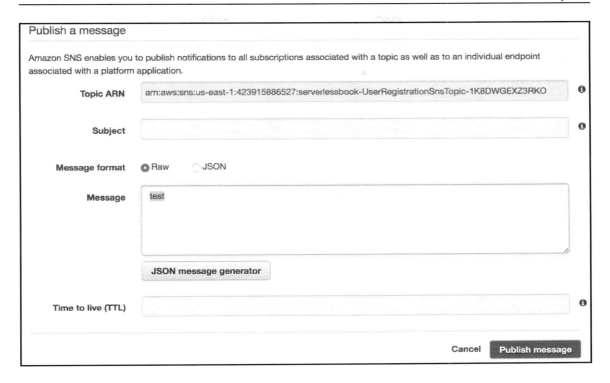

If you go back to RequestBin, you will see that SNS notified it and you can read your message there.

In our architecture, our user registration Lambda will publish the email address of the created user as a message, and this information will be available to the topic's subscribers.

Before we go any further with our code, we must first alter our Lambda's IAM permissions to allow us to publish to that topic.

Add the following block to the Statement array of LambdaCustomPolicy:

```
{
    "Effect": "Allow",
    "Action": [
      "SNS:Publish"
    ],
    "Resource": [
      {
        "Ref": "UserRegistrationSnsTopic"
      }
    ]
}
```

Now, we have to pass the topic's ARN to the Lambda function as an environment variable. Add this environment variable to the environment variables of `UserRegistrationLambda`:

```
"UserRegistrationSnsTopic": {
  "Ref":"UserRegistrationSnsTopic"
}
```

Now, we can add SNS SDK to user registration Lambda. Basically, add this dependency to the `build.gradle` file of `lambda-userregistration`:

```
compile group: 'com.amazonaws', name: 'aws-java-sdk-sns', version: '1.11.+'
```

We can now add the required code to the `Handler` method of this Lambda:

```
private static final Logger LOGGER = Logger.getLogger(Handler.class);
private AmazonSNSClient amazonSNSClient;

@Inject
public Handler setAmazonSNSClient(AmazonSNSClient amazonSNSClient) {
    this.amazonSNSClient = amazonSNSClient;
    return this;
}

private void notifySnsSubscribers(User user) {
  try {
     amazonSNSClient.publish(System.getenv("UserRegistrationSnsTopic"),
       user.getEmail());
     LOGGER.info("SNS notification sent for "+user.getEmail());
  } catch (Exception anyException) {
     LOGGER.info("SNS notification failed for "+user.getEmail(),
       anyException);
  }
}
```

It is a very simple method, and note that we are injecting `AmazonSNSClient` via dependency injection with its default configuration. We might need a custom configured client, and in this case, we would have to configure it in our dependency injection module. However, right now, it is not in the scope of our book, so we will directly use the default configuration.

Finally, we can add this method to the current `handleRequest` method as follows:

```
@Override
public RegistrationOutput handleRequest(RegistrationInput input, Context
context) {
  User createdUser = userService.registerNewUser(input.username,
```

```
  input.email);
    notifySnsSubscribers(createdUser);
    return new RegistrationOutput(createdUser);
}
```

Now, we can deploy our project and create a new user like we showed in the previous chapter. Open the RequestBin page again. You should be seeing that the registered user's email is there, published to the topic.

Consuming the SNS message and sending emails

As the last step, let's create a Lambda function that will subscribe to our topic and send a welcome mail. As usual, let's create our module and the package:

```
$ mkdir -p lambda-userregistration-welcomemail/src/main/
  java/com/serverlessbook/lambda/userregistration/welcomemail
```

Then, let's add the package into the settings.gradle file:

```
echo "include 'lambda-userregistration-welcomemail'" >>
  settings.gradle
```

Let's first create the build.gradle file in our new module and add the required dependencies:

```
dependencies {
  compile group: 'com.amazonaws', name: 'aws-lambda-java-events',
    version: '1.3.0'
  compile group: 'com.amazonaws', name: 'aws-java-sdk-ses',
    version: '1.11.+'compile group: 'com.google.inject',
    name: 'guice', version: guiceVersion
}
```

Then, let's create our Handler class:

```
public class Handler implements RequestHandler<SNSEvent, Void> {
  private static final Injector INJECTOR = Guice.createInjector();
  private static final Logger LOGGER = Logger.getLogger(Handler.class);
  private AmazonSimpleEmailServiceClient simpleEmailServiceClient;

  @Inject
  public Handler setSimpleEmailServiceClient(
      AmazonSimpleEmailServiceClient simpleEmailServiceClient) {
```

```
      this.simpleEmailServiceClient = simpleEmailServiceClient;
      return this;
    }

  public Handler() {
    INJECTOR.injectMembers(this);
    Objects.nonNull(simpleEmailServiceClient);
  }

  private void sendEmail(final String emailAddress) {
    Destination destination = new Destination().
    withToAddresses(emailAddress);

    Message message = new Message()
      .withBody(new Body().withText(new Content("Welcome to our forum!")))
      .withSubject(new Content("Welcome!"));

    try {
      LOGGER.debug("Sending welcome mail to " + emailAddress);
      simpleEmailServiceClient.sendEmail(new SendEmailRequest()
        .withDestination(destination)
        .withSource(System.getenv("SenderEmail"))
        .withMessage(message)
      );
      LOGGER.debug("Sending welcome mail to " + emailAddress +
        " succeeded");
    } catch (Exception anyException) {
      LOGGER.error("Sending welcome mail to " + emailAddress + " failed: ",
        anyException);
    }
  }

  @Override
  public Void handleRequest(SNSEvent input, Context context) {
    input.getRecords().forEach(snsMessage ->
      sendEmail(snsMessage.getSNS().getMessage()));
    return null;
  }
}
```

Here, you should pay attention to a couple of things. First of all, we did not want our custom Lambda handler but the standard one because we do not need any custom JSON deserialization. Here, we used the standard AWS library, `aws-lambda-java-events`, which includes some POJOs for AWS service events. SNSEvent is one of them, which is created in accordance with SNS' event structure. AWS does not provide this type of library in other platforms, but as we are in Java, we are lucky. So, we do not have to worry about parsing the incoming request, and we can directly consume the incoming Java object.

The second thing to pay attention to is how we iterate over the `getRecords()` method of the SNSEvent object. In most cases, this method will return a list of one element, because in theory for each SNS event, only one Lambda invocation is created. However, there are some people reporting that they received more than one message in the same Lambda invocation. It means, it is not sure nor documented that SNS will send only one SNS message per Lambda invocation. Because of this just in case we iterate over the array, instead of just picking the first element of the array.

The last thing to look at is how we build the SES API request. There are a lot of different options here that you can configure. You can check the SES documentation for deeper knowledge, but our configuration just does its job now and sends a raw text mail.

Before we go any further, let's add the required permission to our Lambda's IAM permission:

```
{
  "Effect": "Allow",
  "Action": [
    "ses:*"
  ],
  "Resource": "*"
}
```

Then, let's create the Lambda function with the `SenderEmail` environment variable. You have to change the variable for your configuration, so you can add any email address belonging to the domain you verified on the SES panel:

```
"UserRegistrationWelcomeMailLambda": {
  "Type": "AWS::Lambda::Function",
  "Properties": {
    "Handler": "com.serverlessbook.lambda.
      userregistration.welcomemail.Handler",
    "Runtime": "java8",
    "Timeout": "300",
    "MemorySize": "1024",
    "Description": "User registration welcome mail Lambda",
    "Role": {
      "Fn::GetAtt": [
        "LambdaExecutionRole",
        "Arn"
      ]
    },
    "Code": {
      "S3Bucket": {
```

```
                "Ref": "DeploymentBucket"
            },
            "S3Key": {
              "Fn::Sub": "artifacts/lambda-userregistration-welcomemail/
                ${ProjectVersion}/${DeploymentTime}.jar"
            }
          },
          "Environment": {
            "Variables": {
              "SenderEmail": "info@example.com"
            }
          }
        }
      }
    },
    "UserRegistrationWelcomeMailLambdaPermission": {
      "Type": "AWS::Lambda::Permission",
        "Properties": {
          "Action": "lambda:InvokeFunction",
          "FunctionName": {
            "Ref": "UserRegistrationWelcomeMailLambda"
          },
          "Principal": "sns.amazonaws.com",
          "SourceArn": {
            "Fn::Sub": "arn:aws:sns:${AWS::Region}:${AWS::AccountId}:*"
          }
        }
      }
    }
```

The second part of this block was the Lambda permission to let SNS invoke our function. As you remember from the API Gateway part, we should let AWS services invoke our Lambda functions to achieve execution of them on behalf of us. As we did for the API Gateway, here we allow sns.amazonaws.com to identify to execute our Lambda function.

As the last step, we must add a new subscription to UserRegistrationSnsTopic. Let's add this block to the Subscriptions part of UserRegistrationSnsTopic:

```
{
  "Endpoint": {
    "Fn::GetAtt": [
      "UserRegistrationWelcomeMailLambda",
      "Arn"
    ]
  },
  "Protocol": "lambda"
}
```

Everything is ready to be run now.

Just try to register a new user with the following command, changing the domain name to yours:

```
$ curl  -X POST  -H "Content-Type: application/json" -d
  '{"username": "tester3", email: "success@simulator.amazonses.com"}'
  -v https://serverlessbook.example.com/users
```

You can check the logs of your Lambda function to see that they are triggered via SNS and send the email to the user!

Integrating a messaging queue

SNS is a messaging system following the Pub/Sub pattern where you fire a message from one source and consume from many resources parallely. On the other hand, the other important messaging systems are queues, where you can fire messages from multiple sources and consume them from single or multiple consumers, but one by one.

AWS also provides such a service called **SQS (Simple Queue Service)**. In SQS, you create queues and send messages to them. After that, you can poll messages to your customer and consume them. Before we finish this chapter, we can also see briefly how we can use SQS in our application. However, we will not consume the messages we will push to the queue we will create. Our application does not have such a use case, and to consume SQS messages, you need to have an always up and running consumer component installed on a normal instance.

In this section, we will replicate the messages from SNS to SQS. We've already created a SNS topic for registered users. We can also set the SQS topic as a subscriber to our topic, so whatever notification that comes to SNS will be also stored at the SQS queue. After that, it is up to you to consume those messages or not. SQS automatically deletes messages that have been in a queue for more than maximum message retention period. The default value for the retention period is 4 days. However, you can set the message retention period to a value from 60 seconds to 1,209,600 seconds (14 days).

First, let's create our queue and the policy attached to it:

```
"UserRegistrationQueue": {
  "Type": "AWS::SQS::Queue"
},
"UserRegistrationQueuePolicy": {
  "Type": "AWS::SQS::QueuePolicy",
  "Properties": {
    "PolicyDocument": {
      "Version": "2012-10-17",
      "Statement": [
```

```
        {
          "Effect": "Allow",
          "Principal": "*",
          "Action": "SQS:SendMessage",
          "Resource": {
            "Fn::GetAtt": [
              "UserRegistrationQueue",
              "Arn"
            ]
          },
          "Condition": {
            "ArnEquals": {
              "aws:SourceArn": {
                "Ref": "UserRegistrationSnsTopic"
              }
            }
          }
        }
      ]
    },
    "Queues": [
      {
        "Ref": "UserRegistrationQueue"
      }
    ]
  }
}
```

AWS::SQS::Queue has a lot of options for fine-tuning and also dead letter queues, and you should adjust them according to your needs, but with the default options, it will just work. The dead letter queue is a concept which many queue systems implement and it is intended to store messages which are not successfully processed in normal ways. So, you can use dead letter queues as a error recovery system.

The second resource adds an access policy to the queue. Just like Lambdas, we need to let SQS know that another identity, SNS in this case, wants to access to it for publishing messages. That's why we allow the SQS:SendMessage permission to SNS if the incoming message belongs to our topic's ARN.

As the last step, we will add the following subscription definition to Subscription to the UserRegistrationSnsTopic resource:

```
{
  "Endpoint": {
    "Fn::GetAtt": [
      "UserRegistrationQueue",
      "Arn"
```

```
        ]
    },
    "Protocol": "sqs"
}
```

After deploying our application, we can navigate to the SQS section of the AWS Console and see our queue there.

You can click on the queue and **Queue Actions** and then on the **View/Delete Messages** button. A new window will open where you can see the incoming messages to your queue:

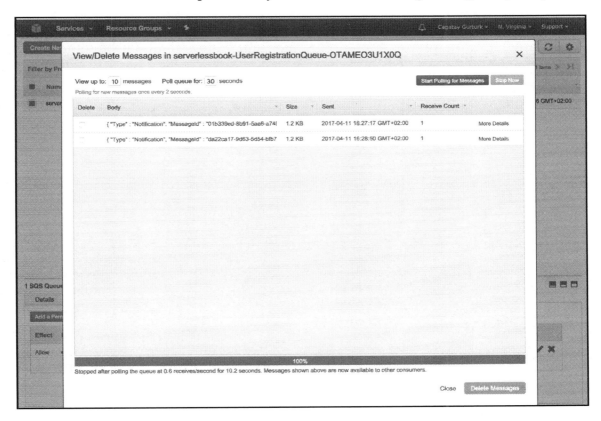

Now, you can create a new user via your API and see that the information about new users is arriving to your queue.

Summary

Congratulations! As promised, you built a fully working image upload and resize endpoint with an incredibly low amount of code. After that, we built a loosely coupled software component that is triggered via events in the cloud and executed operations.

Obviously, our software has room to improve. So far, we drew a reference architecture for our software, and it is now your task to fill in the missing parts and develop the software further. Quite often, it is not possible to cover all the features and configuration options the AWS offers. Actually, the platform is evolving so fast that if we had covered all aspects, everything would have become outdated in a short time. You should read the AWS documentation carefully to find out how to implement the architecture you have in your mind. There's definitely a way to do it.

Our journey does not end here. In the next chapter, we will introduce you to the CloudSearch service, which is a managed Elasticsearch service. We will notify CloudSearch when a new user is registered via SNS and also create a basic search endpoint to search our users by email.

7
Searching Data

In the last chapter, we saw how to build surrounding services around our serverless application with minimal custom code usage. In this chapter, we will also develop a supporting service which is search. Content is the king, and it is very important to help your users discover the most relevant content in your application.

Search is a huge topic that many books can be written about, but in this chapter, we wanted to show one of the AWS offerings that lets you build a simple search engine: **CloudSearch**. CloudSearch is a fully managed service built on top of SOLR and provides a simple API to index and search documents, as well as build a suggestion feature.

If your needs are more complex, you may consider using the **ElasticSearch** service. This is managed Elasticsearch cluster provisioning server, but in this case, you would be using AWS APIs just to provision your cluster. All the communication between your software and Elasticsearch cluster would be via Elasticsearch's REST API or native library.

CloudSearch, on the other hand, provides an API (and of course SDKs in different languages) that isolates the complexity of the underlying search infrastructure, so you can easily index and search documents.

In this chapter, we will create our search domain and then create a new Lambda function that indexes each user who is registered into the search domain. Finally, we will create another endpoint in our API that consumes the documents, so it autocompletes the usernames of registered users. Throughout the chapter we will cover the following topics:

- Creating and configuring a search domain with CloudSearch
- Creating an API Gateway endpoint to proxy CloudSearch's autocomplete endpoint
- Updating the search index when a new data comes into our system.

Creating the search domain

As a first step, we should create the search domain. A **search domain** is a cluster of machines in which we store our documents.

To create a search domain, first, we need to navigate to the CloudSearch section of the AWS Console and click on the **Create a New Domain** button.

After pressing this button, a new wizard will launch that will walk you through the new search domain creation. You should specify a name for your search domain, and in our case, we name it serverlessbook:

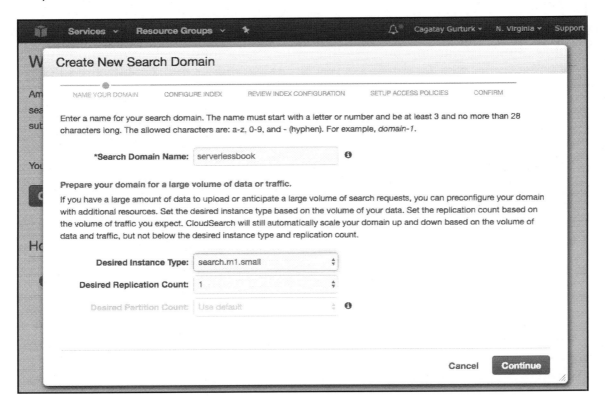

On the same screen, you should also specify an instance type. So far, we never had to specify any instance type, but CloudSearch is not fully serverless, so you will be launching virtual machines under the hood. CloudSearch has a family of instances starting from `search.m1.small` to `search.m3.2xlarge`. These instances have different hardware configurations and different pricing per hour. For our example, we will pick the smallest instance, `search.m1.small`, and also set **Desired Replication Count** as **1**. We will also set **Desired Partition Count** to **1** for the exercise.

 Be aware that once you create a search domain, your account will start to be charged per hour. AWS provides a trial period for new accounts, so you may use it for free for a limited amount of time, but still, it is a good idea to turn off the search domain once you finish the exercises.

When we click on the **Continue** button, we are prompted to configure our index for the search domain. AWS gives us some options to analyze the current documents to predict an indexing structure, but here, we will choose the **Manual Configuration** option to customize our indexed fields in documents:

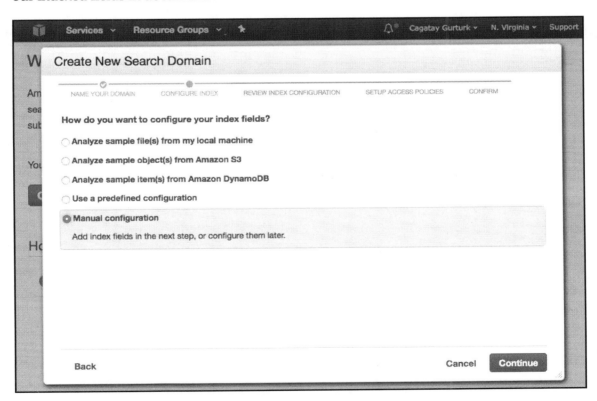

On the next screen, we are prompted to enter indexable fields in our document:

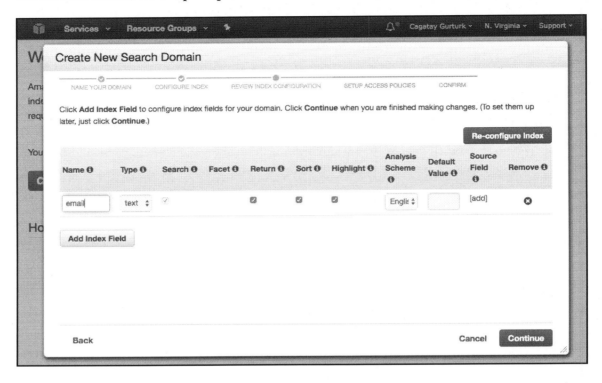

Here, we add `email`, `userid`, and `username` as indexable fields and select **text** as **Type** for all the items. Note that we have more options here, such as numeric or date value, but as we only have string values in our users table, we select **text**.

At the start of the wizard, we could also select **Analyze sample item(s) from Amazon DynamoDB** and let CloudSearch decide about indexable fields in the domain. However, we wanted to show you how to do the configuration manually, so we did not go that way.

Like all AWS services, we have to define an access policy for CloudSearch also. On the next screen, we can select one of the predefined policies or write our own:

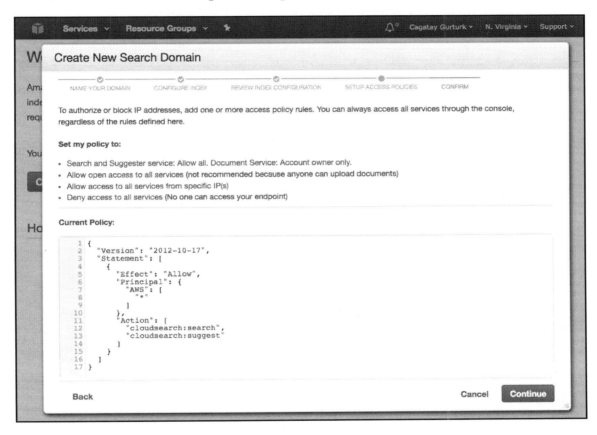

For the sake of simplicity, we will write the following policy to the box:

```
{
  "Version": "2012-10-17",
  "Statement": [
    {
      "Effect": "Allow",
      "Principal": {
        "AWS": [
          "*"
        ]
      },
      "Action": [
        "cloudsearch:search",
        "cloudsearch:suggest"
      ]
    }
  ]
}
```

This policy allows public access for the Search and Suggester service, but only allows the current AWS owner to upload documents.

After this step, you'll be prompted to confirm all the configurations and create the search domain by clicking on the **Confirm** button. It will take up to 10 minutes to launch your search domain and bring it online.

Uploading test data

We can now directly upload some documents from DynamoDB to the CloudSearch domain, so we can directly try out our new search engine.

CloudSearch provides another wizard for that purpose, which can be accessed from the domain's dashboard:

To launch the wizard, you can click on the **Upload Documents** button. After that, you'll see a couple of options:

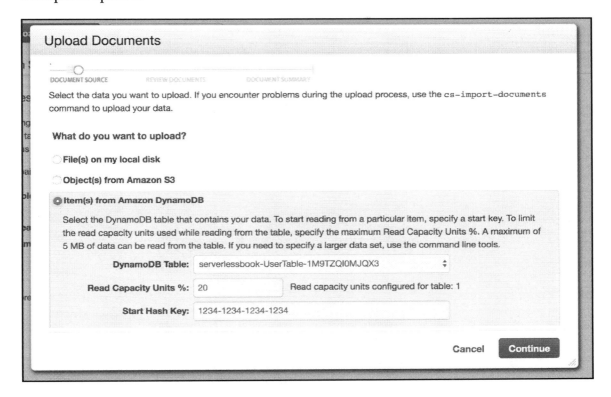

We should select the **Item(s) from Amazon DynamoDB** option to proceed with DynamoDB and then click on **Continue**. In the next step, a sample from our table will be read and analyzed against index structure. As all the fields we have in the user table are also indexed in the CloudSearch table, there should not be any problem:

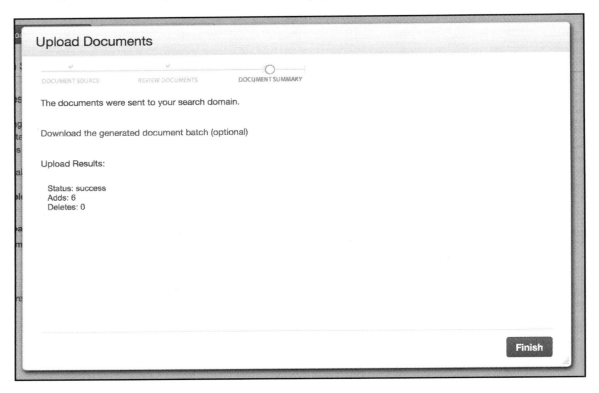

When we finish the wizard, the result will be successful, and CloudSearch will index all the users that we created in our API during the tests.

Let's run a test query to ensure that our data is already there.

You can click on **Run a Test Search** on the left column and access a panel where you can test your search queries:

In the previous chapter, we created a user with the `success@simulator.amazonses.com` email address. If we can write it to the **Search** field and click on **Go**, the result should appear, meaning that our data is now indexed by CloudSearch.

On the other hand, uploading documents manually is not a production-grade operation, and it should be automatized. That's why, in the upcoming sections of this chapter, we will create a small Lambda function that reads the data from the SNS topic and writes to CloudSearch.

Creating the suggester

Suggesters are one of the coolest features of CloudSearch that you can use to build an autocomplete system. We will create a suggester for the username field so that we can use it in a search field for our forum application.

To create a suggester, click on the **Suggesters** link on the left column and then on the **Add Suggester** button:

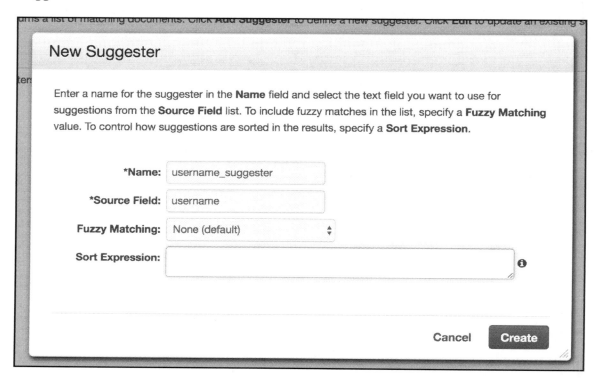

Here, you have to give a name to the suggester (we set username_suggester in our case) and a source field to create the suggester from. You can also select the **Fuzzy Matching** option that will tolerate typo errors and bring more similar results even though the keyword does not start with the given parameter.

After creating the suggester, CloudSearch should again index the documents, but as we do not have many documents at the moment, it should not take a lot of time.

Creating the API endpoint for suggestions

You may think that to expose search results, we would need another Lambda function. On the other hand, in our API endpoint, we just need the document we saved to CloudSearch, and we can directly expose it to the client. Then, we can use the similar method we used for the S3 upload and use API Gateway as a proxy between CloudSearch's AWS API and our publicly facing API.

To create such an API, let's first create a resource in the /search path using the method we already know from the earlier steps. Let's add this block to the Resources block in our CloudFormation template:

```
"SearchResource": {
  "Type": "AWS::ApiGateway::Resource",
  "Properties": {
    "PathPart": "search",
    "RestApiId": {
      "Ref": "RestApi"
    },
    "ParentId": {
      "Fn::GetAtt": [
        "RestApi",
        "RootResourceId"
      ]
    }
  }
}
```

To integrate CloudSearch with API Gateway, we will need to know the automatically generated subdomain for the CloudSearch domain. When you look at the CloudSearch dashboard, you will see this value under the Search Endpoint title. For example, this value can be shown as follows:

search-serverlessbook-uiyqpdvcdz7o4hxudtnqzpjdtu.us-east-1.cloudsearch.amazonaws.com

We need only the first portion, so add search-serverlessbook-uiyqpdvcdz7o4hxudtnqzpjdtu as a parameter in our CloudFormation template. Let's create this parameter value to be used in the next part:

```
"CloudSearchDomain": {
  "Type": "String",
  "Description": "Endpoint Name for CloudSearch domain"
}
```

Do not forget to set this parameter to your endpoint's value in `build.gradle`! You have to omit the `search-` prefix when you write the parameter to your `build.gradle` file. As you can see on the dashboard, CloudSearch provides two endpoints for different purposes: **Search Endpoint** and **Document Endpoint**. For example, for this configuration, the endpoints are:

> Search Endpoint: search-serverlessbook-uiyqpdvcdz7o4hxudtnqzpjdtu.us-east-1.cloudsearch.amazonaws.com
>
> Document Endpoint: doc-serverlessbook-uiyqpdvcdz7o4hxudtnqzpjdtu.us-east-1.cloudsearch.amazonaws.com

You should write `serverlessbook-uiyqpdvcdz7o4hxudtnqzpjdtu` to your `build.gradle` file, so for different purposes, we will populate different endpoints in our code.

Now, we can create the most complicated part, the method itself. Let's first add the code and then analyze the important parts of it:

```
"SearchGetMethod": {
  "Type": "AWS::ApiGateway::Method",
  "Properties": {
    "HttpMethod": "GET",
    "RestApiId": {
      "Ref": "RestApi"
    },
    "ResourceId": {
      "Ref": "SearchResource"
    },
    "RequestParameters": {
      "method.request.querystring.q": "q"
    },
    "AuthorizationType": "NONE",
      "Integration": {
        "Type": "AWS",
        "Uri": {
          "Fn::Sub":"arn:aws:apigateway:${AWS::Region}:search-
          ${CloudSearchDomain}.cloudsearch:path//2013-01-01/suggest"
        },
        "IntegrationHttpMethod": "GET",
        "Credentials": {
          "Fn::GetAtt": [
            "ApiGatewayProxyRole",
            "Arn"
          ]
        },
        "RequestParameters": {
          "integration.request.querystring.suggester":
```

```
                "'username_suggester'",
            "integration.request.querystring.q":
                "method.request.querystring.q"
        },
        "RequestTemplates": {
        },
        "PassthroughBehavior": "WHEN_NO_TEMPLATES",
        "IntegrationResponses": [
            {
                "SelectionPattern": ".*",
                "StatusCode": "200"
            }
        ]
    },
    "MethodResponses": [
        {
            "StatusCode": "200"
        }
    ]
}
}
```

This is pretty similar to S3 integration. Here, we do not force authentication, because we want our `Search` API to be public. You could, of course, change it easily according to your needs, just adding authorization Lambda to the configuration.

Maybe, the most important configuration is the `Uri` field, where we set which AWS API we should send our request to. Here, we will construct the full path using the `AWS::Region` and `CloudSearchDomain` parameters. Note that we have prepended `search-` to the subdomain to construct the URL you read in the CloudSearch dashboard. You may wonder what `/2013-01-01/suggest` means. This is the documented API endpoint for suggestion. If you check the documentation at `http://docs.aws.amazon.com/cloudsearch/latest/developerguide/search-api.html#suggest`, you can see this information and more endpoints.

It is always a good idea to check documentation to find out which URL to write when you are constructing your API. Alternatively, you can create the method using the API Gateway Console, and it will construct the URI for you. Once you create the method using this way, you can check its configuration via the AWS CLI and you will see which path is constructed by the Console. Then, you can use this value in your CloudFormation template.

As you might have noted, this CloudSearch API endpoint expects the `suggester` and `q` parameters. We get the second parameter from the client, because it is what they search on our application. On the other hand, we can add the `suggester` parameter at the API Gateway level and pass the request to CloudSearch API. That's why we pass `'username_suggester'` (with quotes) to `integration.request.querystring.suggester` and `integration.request.querystring.q` to `method.request.querystring.q`.

As a last step, we have to add `SearchGetMethod` to the `DependsOn` collection of `ApiDeployment` to prevent our API from being deployed before the method's creation:

```
"ApiDeployment": {
  "DependsOn": [
    "TestGetMethod",
    "SearchGetMethod"
  ],
```

Now, we can deploy the API and see the results under the `/search?q=keyword` query.

Lambda function for updating search data

Now, we will create another Lambda function that reads the SNS notification and writes the value to CloudSearch. Unfortunately, at this stage, we need to refactor our code a bit because as you remember, we were publishing only the email addresses of the newly registered users to the SNS. We now need to change the user registration Lambda to emit the user data as a JSON value.

To accomplish this, let's first modify our `User` object in `User Service` with Jackson annotations to have a correct serialization to JSON.

Change the `com.serverlessbook.services.user.domain.User` class and add the following the `@JsonProperty` annotations to all properties:

```
@DynamoDBHashKey(attributeName = "UserId")
@JsonProperty("userid")
private String id;

@DynamoDBIndexHashKey(globalSecondaryIndexName =
  "UsernameIndex", attributeName = "Username")
@JsonProperty("username")
private String username;

@DynamoDBIndexHashKey(globalSecondaryIndexName = "EmailIndex",
```

```
        attributeName = "Email")
    @JsonProperty("email")
    private String email;
```

Then, we can change `User Registration Lambda` and add the JSON serialization logic there:

```
private void notifySnsSubscribers(User user) {
    try { amazonSNSClient.publish(System.getenv("UserRegistrationSnsTopic"),
        new ObjectMapper().writeValueAsString(user));
        LOGGER.info("SNS notification sent for "+user.getEmail());
    } catch (Exception anyException) {
        LOGGER.info("SNS notification failed for "+user.getEmail(),
        anyException);
    }
}
```

You might consider separating JSON serialization and deserialization to another service, but for the sake of simplicity, we leave it like this.

Modifying the welcome mail sender Lambda

As we mentioned at the beginning, we have to also modify the Lambda function we used to send the welcome mail to the process user object as JSON instead of an email address as plain text. First, we have to add the `services-user` subproject to this Lambda's compile dependencies so that it can see the `User` class that will be sent in the SNS payload.

Then, we can change the `sendMail(final String emailAddress)` method to accept `User` as a parameter:

```
private void sendEmail(final User user) {
    final String emailAddress = user.getEmail();
    Destination destination = new
Destination().withToAddresses(emailAddress);

    Message message = new Message()
      .withBody(new Body().withText(new Content("Welcome to our forum!")))
      .withSubject(new Content("Welcome!"));

    try {
      LOGGER.debug("Sending welcome mail to " + emailAddress);
      simpleEmailServiceClient.sendEmail(new SendEmailRequest()
        .withDestination(destination)
        .withSource(System.getenv("SenderEmail"))
        .withMessage(message)
```

```
    );
    LOGGER.debug("Sending welcome mail to " + emailAddress + " succeeded");
  } catch (Exception anyException) {
    LOGGER.error("Sending welcome mail to " + emailAddress + " failed: ",
      anyException);
  }
}
```

Then, we can change the SNS handler to convert the string to JSON:

```
@Override
public Void handleRequest(SNSEvent input, Context context) {
  input.getRecords().forEach(snsMessage -> {
    try {
      sendEmail(new
ObjectMapper().readValue(snsMessage.getSNS().getMessage(),
        User.class));
    } catch (IOException anyException) {
      LOGGER.error("JSON could not be deserialized", anyException);
    }
  });
  return null;
}
```

Here, it smells a bit of bad code. We will create another Lambda function that will consume the SNS event and deserialize JSON. We can't repeat the code always for different functions. So, let's create a new type of handler in our main Lambda that we can use with the SNS consumer functions.

Let's first remove the compile group, `'com.amazonaws',  name:  'aws-lambda-java-events',  version:  '1.3.0'` dependency from the welcome mail lambda and add it to our generic `lambda` package.

Then, let's create a `SnsLambdaHandler<I>` class in the same package:

```
public abstract class SnsLambdaHandler<I> implements
RequestHandler<SNSEvent, Void> {

  private static final Logger LOGGER =
    Logger.getLogger(SnsLambdaHandler.class);
  private final ObjectMapper objectMapper;
  protected SnsLambdaHandler() {
    objectMapper=new ObjectMapper();
  }

  public abstract void handleSnsRequest(I input, Context context);
```

```
@SuppressWarnings("unchecked")
private Class<I> getJsonType() {
  return (Class<I>) ((ParameterizedType)
   getClass().getGenericSuperclass()).getActualTypeArguments()[0];
}

@Override
public Void handleRequest(SNSEvent input, Context context) {
  input.getRecords().forEach(snsMessage -> {
    try {
      I deserializedPayload =
        objectMapper.readValue(snsMessage.getSNS().getMessage(),
          getJsonType());
      handleSnsRequest(deserializedPayload, context);
    } catch (IOException anyException) {
      LOGGER.error("JSON could not be deserialized", anyException);
    }
  });
  return null;
}
}
```

As you can see, this abstract class now requires its children to implement the
`handleSnsRequest(I input, Context context)` method, and before invoking it, it
deserializes the payload inside the SNS message to whatever class its children require in
generics.

Now, we can simplify the welcome mail handler, extending it from the
`SnsLambdaHandler<User>` class and implementing the abstract method from its parent.
So, it becomes as follows:

```
public class Handler extends SnsLambdaHandler<User> {
  ...
  @Override
  public void handleSnsRequest(User input, Context context) {
    sendEmail(input);
  }
}
```

We have a more object-oriented structure now, and we separated the deserialization logic
from the Lambda's handler itself.

Creating the Lambda function to update CloudSearch

Now, we can create the Lambda function that will save the user information to CloudSearch. As usual, let's create our subproject and package:

```
$ mkdir -p lambda-userregistration-cloudsearch/com/
  serverlessbook/lambda/userregistration/search
```

Then, we can add this to our `settings.gradle` file to be recognized by the main project:

```java
public class Handler extends SnsLambdaHandler<User> {
    private static final Injector INJECTOR = Guice.createInjector();
    private static final Logger LOGGER = Logger.getLogger(Handler.class);
    private AmazonCloudSearchDomainClient amazonCloudSearchDomainClient;
    private final ObjectMapper objectMapper = new ObjectMapper();

    @Inject
    public Handler setAmazonCloudSearchDomainClient(
      AmazonCloudSearchDomainClient amazonCloudSearchDomainClient) {
        this.amazonCloudSearchDomainClient = amazonCloudSearchDomainClient;
        this.amazonCloudSearchDomainClient.setEndpoint(System.getenv("
          CloudSearchDomain"));
        return this;
    }

    public Handler() {
        INJECTOR.injectMembers(this);
        Objects.nonNull(amazonCloudSearchDomainClient);
    }

    private void uploadDocument(User user) {
        try {
            final Map<String, Object> documentRequest = new HashMap<>();
            documentRequest.put("type", "add");
            documentRequest.put("id", user.getId());
            documentRequest.put("fields", user);
            LOGGER.info("User with id " + user.getId() + " is being uploaded to
              CloudSearch");
            byte[] jsonAsByteStream = objectMapper.writeValueAsBytes(new Map[]
              {documentRequest});
            if (jsonAsByteStream != null) {
                ByteArrayInputStream document = new ByteArrayInputStream(
                  jsonAsByteStream);
                amazonCloudSearchDomainClient.uploadDocuments(new
                  UploadDocumentsRequest()
                  .withDocuments(document)
```

```
          .withContentLength((long) document.available())
          .withContentType(ContentType.Applicationjson)
        );
      }
    } catch (JsonProcessingException jsonProcessingException) {
      LOGGER.error("Object could not be converted to JSON",
        jsonProcessingException);
    } catch (Exception anyException) {
      LOGGER.error("Upload was failing", anyException);
    }
  }

  @Override
  public void handleSnsRequest(User input, Context context) {
    uploadDocument(input);
  }
}
```

From the SNS point of view, this function is very similar to the previous welcome mail function. Note the line in the constructor:

```
this.amazonCloudSearchDomainClient.setEndpoint(
  System.getenv("CloudSearchDomain"));
```

Amazon SDK requires you to specify the endpoint because every CloudSearch deployment has a different endpoint, as we mentioned earlier, and API requests should be sent to those endpoints. Actually, AWS is installing its own software to every search instance you are running in your account.

Inside the uploadDocument method, we will create the JSON that this endpoint expects. CloudSearch has a batch upload API that expects the following form of input:

```
[
  {
    "id": "1234-1234-1234",
    "type": "add",
    "fields": {
      "userid":"1234-1234-1234",
      "email": "test@test.com",
      "username": "test_user"
    }
  }
]
```

As you might have noted, it expects an array of documents, with the `type`, `id`, and `fields` keys as mandatory. In the type field, you can specify `add` and `delete` to add or remove documents. Each searchable document should be identified with an ID (in our case, we use the user ID for this value), and in the `fields` key, you should specify the fields you configured to be searched and their content.

The rest of the method is pretty simple. We create an InputStream from this object structure to create the required JSON using Jackson.

Of course, for this project, we have to create a `build.gradle` file and add the required dependencies, including the CloudSearch SDK:

```
dependencies {
  compile group: 'com.google.inject', name: 'guice', version: guiceVersion
  compile project(':services-user')
  compile group: 'com.amazonaws', name: 'aws-java-sdk-cloudsearch',
    version: '1.11.+'
}
```

Creating and configuring the Lambda function with CloudFormation

Now, we can create the Lambda function in our CloudFormation file:

```
"UserRegistrationCloudSearchLambda": {
    "Type": "AWS::Lambda::Function",
    "Properties": {
      "Handler": "com.serverlessbook.lambda.userregistration.search.Handler",
      "Runtime": "java8",
      "Timeout": "300",
      "MemorySize": "1024",
      "Description": "User Registration Search Lambda",
      "Role": {
        "Fn::GetAtt": [
          "LambdaExecutionRole",
          "Arn"
        ]
      },
      "Code": {
        "S3Bucket": {
          "Ref": "DeploymentBucket"
        },
        "S3Key": {
          "Fn::Sub": "artifacts/lambda-userregistration-cloudsearch/
```

```
            ${ProjectVersion}/${DeploymentTime}.jar"
        }
    },
    "Environment": {
        "Variables": {
            "CloudSearchDomain": {
                "Fn::Sub": "doc-${CloudSearchDomain}.${AWS::Region}.
                    cloudsearch.amazonaws.com"
            }
        }
    }
}
}
}
```

Note that we prepended `doc-` to construct the document endpoint of CloudSearch and inject it into our Lambda function as an environment variable named `CloudSearchDomain`.

To integrate this function with SNS, we have to give permission to SNS to invoke the function, and we do this exactly how we did with the previous function:

```
"UserRegistrationCloudSearchLambdaPermission": {
    "Type": "AWS::Lambda::Permission",
    "Properties": {
        "Action": "lambda:InvokeFunction",
        "FunctionName": {
            "Ref": "UserRegistrationCloudSearchLambda"
        },
        "Principal": "sns.amazonaws.com","SourceArn": {
            "Fn::Sub": "arn:aws:sns:${AWS::Region}:${AWS::AccountId}:*"
        }
    }
}
```

Finally, we will add the Lambda to our SNS topic as a subscriber:

```
{
    "Endpoint": {
        "Fn::GetAtt": [
            "UserRegistrationCloudSearchLambda",
            "Arn"
        ]
    },
    "Protocol": "lambda"
}
```

We're done. Now, we can deploy our stack, and all the new users who registered to our application will be also indexed in CloudSearch.

You can now register a new user using the user registration endpoint, executing the same command from previous chapters. Once you register the user, you can query your endpoint at /search path with the q parameter and a result should appear.

Alternatively, you can use the CloudSearch dashboard to execute a query against the search domain and ensure that data flow is working without any problem.

Summary

Search is a huge topic that many books can be written about. On the other hand, in this chapter, we wanted to introduce an AWS service that can meet your basic search requirements, and more importantly, we wanted to show how you can separate different parts of your big software into small pieces.

In our Java code, there might be some points to improve, and we did not write a lot of tests. These are parts that you can develop further and practice your skills.

In the next chapter, which is also the last one, we will see some monitoring features for our serverless application.

8
Monitoring, Logging, and Security

As every seasoned software engineer knows, when the development process of a software system ends, the operation efforts start. While we are developing our software, we need to pay maximum attention and once the software is in production, we should monitor the software carefully to detect problems and bottlenecks. Serverless applications are not any different and need to be monitored carefully as well.

Security is also another important aspect that we shouldn't need not to reiterate. Any security problem that our software might have, can cost money and reputation of our business.

In the last chapter, we will see some tools provided by AWS that help to monitor our software and mitigate issues. We will set up automated health checks that will constantly monitor the health of our serverless application, we will extend the topic of logging via CloudWatch, and learn to create automated alarms responding to different situations.

In the last section, we will see how to operate Lambda functions to access protected resources behind a protected AWS network in a **VPC (Virtual Private Cloud)** environment.

We will cover the following topics in this chapter:

- Setting up automated health checks
- Setting up alarm-based pattern matching in application logs
- Running Lambda functions in VPC

Setting up a Route53 health check

We defined serverless applications as highly available applications because-within the SLA-there are always some servers that are available for your functions and they are even scaling up and down according to the capacity you need. On the other hand, it is always good idea to set up a automized health checks, so you can always monitor the health of your application and also you can monitor the latency, so you can make sure that all your endpoints are working properly.

Starting off with the setup

In this section, we will first see how to set up a health check for one of our endpoints with latency graphs. First, we will do this using AWS Console; then we will write a CloudFormation block to produce the same thing.

Let's start our set up by navigating to Route53 AWS Console and clicking **Health Checks** link on the left. It will takes us to a list where all health checks can be seen, which is empty in our case.

You can click the **Create Health Check** button to open the wizard to create a new check:

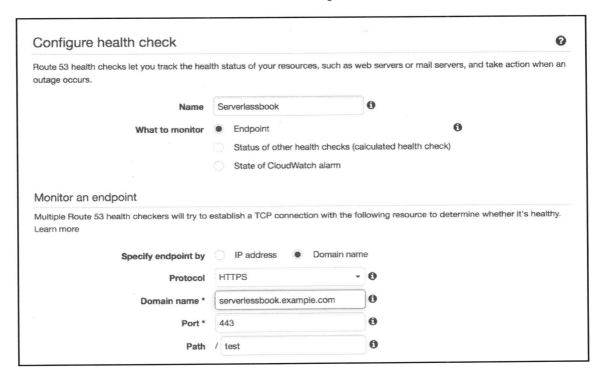

The options here are very trivial. You need to enter **Domain name** and **Path** of health check point. For this example, we will check the /test endpoint.

 Our application is a serverless application; therefore, every endpoint is working independently. That's why it does not make much sense to create only one health check and draw a conclusion that our software is healthy just because that single endpoint is healthy. You'll need to create checks for each endpoint and create an aggregated health check using **Status of other health checks (calculated health check)** afterwards.

On the same screen, you will see the **Advanced configuration** section where you can add a couple of more configuration. For example, you can set a faster interval of checks (with extra price), add a string matching check, and also enable latency graphs using the checkbox. For our example, we only enable **Latency graphs**. Don't disable SNI support because CloudFront uses SNI. If in case you disable it, health checkers won't be able to connect to your application:

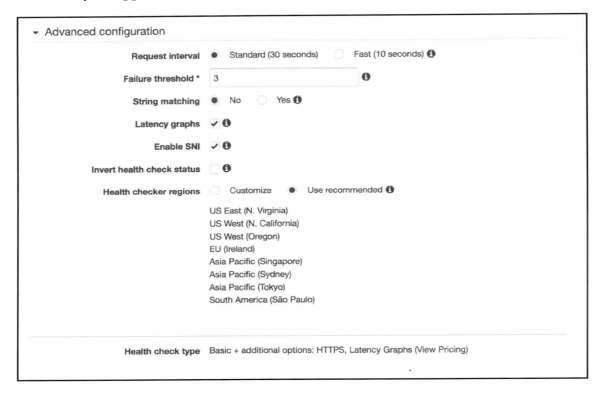

When you click the **Next** button on this screen, you will be asked to create an alarm for this health check. Alarms are a very powerful feature of AWS that help you to take action when a specific event happens in the cloud. For now, we will set up AWS to send us an email when there is an issue with the health check. At this step please check **Yes** for **Create alarm** option. When other options appear, check **New SNS topic**, write a **Topic name**, and fill in the **Recipient email addresses** field:

This wizard will create a couple of AWS resources under the hood that you can also modify for your needs:

- An SNS topic
- Email type subscription for this topic
- A CloudWatch alarm that sends the ALARM and OK states to this SNS topic.

Configuring health checks for email notifications

You are not bound to email notification. As you have already seen, SNS can support a couple of types of endpoint such as SMS, or you can even invoke a Lambda function in case of your health check fails, so you can execute custom code.

After configuring the alarm, we can click on **Create health check** button to finish the wizard.

To be able to receive email messages to your address, you need to go to your inbox and confirm the subscription by clicking on the link in the message you received from AWS.

After creating the alarm, you will see that actually it is failing. To understand the problem, you can click on the alarm and navigate to **Health checkers** tab to see what the underlying issue is:

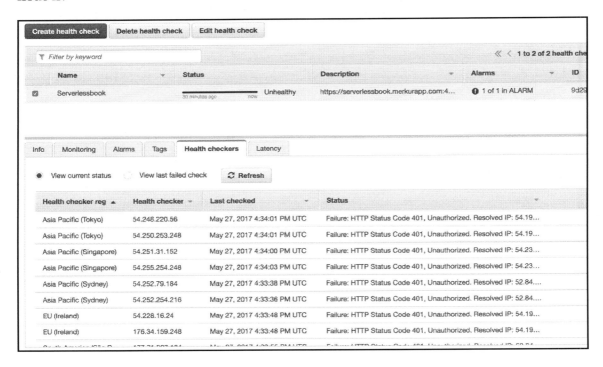

As you can see, health checkers are failing because the endpoint under test needs an authorization header and the health checkers are not sending this value. Ironically it means that our endpoint's authorization works good but still we want to check our application's code, so let's remove the authorization from this endpoint and make the health check pass.

Enabling SMS notifications for health checks

If you want, let's also add SMS notification to your SNS topic, so you can receive alerts even you don't have internet access.

Please navigate to SNS console and find the topic you've just created:

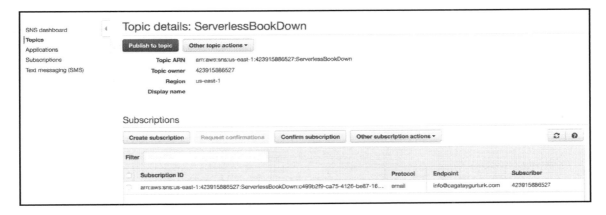

Here you can click the **Create subscription** button, select **SMS** as **Protocol**, and write your phone number in the **Endpoint** field:

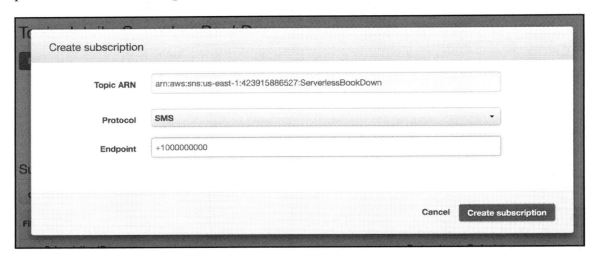

When you create subscription clicking the button, every notification that arrives to this topic will be also delivered to your cell phone via SMS.

Bringing health check to healthy mode

Now we can remove the authorization in `TestGetMethod` by replacing the following CloudFormation template with `"AuthorizationType": "NONE"`:

```
"AuthorizationType": "CUSTOM",
"AuthorizerId": {
  "Ref": "ApiGatewayAuthorizer"
},
```

Go back to the health check console to see if health checkers are now able to access the application.

After a while you will notice that the health check is now in healthy mode but you did not get any message. This is because the wizard sets up the CloudWatch alarm to send the notification only on `ALARM` state. We need to fix this in the next section.

Mastering CloudWatch alarms

Before we see how to fix the issue we had, it is a good idea to understand what are CloudWatch alarms. First of all, CloudWatch is a centric service of AWS that collects and aggregates metrics from different cloud services. Using CloudWatch, we can monitor many types of metric, such as the object count of a S3 bucket, the 5xx error rate of an API Gateway or CloudFront, or the pending item count of a SQS event.

Right now you can navigate to the CloudWatch console, click on the **Metrics** link and explore the existing metrics published for you. For example, in the following screenshot we see the total request count of our CloudFront distribution:

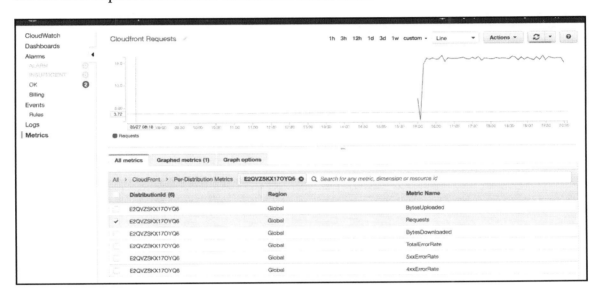

As you can see, the request count increased significantly just after we set up Route53 health check. Before we set it up, our example application was idle, and now there is a flow of requests from different health checkers.

Similarly, you can see the error rate of the API. Instead of requests, let's enable the **4xxErrorRate** metric and you will see this type of graph:

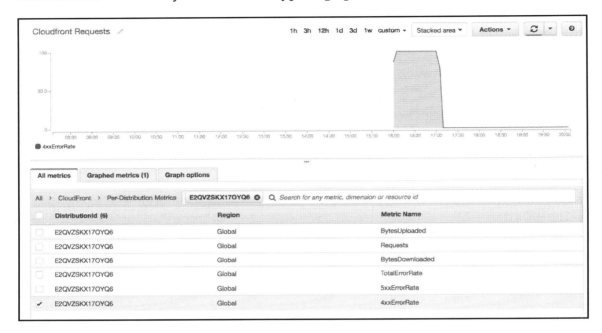

This is because when we first set up the health check, we had authorization for the tested endpoint. After we fixed the issue, the error rate decreased significantly.

This is a very powerful feature and it comes out of box. For an on-premise solution, you would need to install some logging solutions, such as **Logstash** for aggregating logs and **Kibana** for exploring them visually. However, most of the functionality of that stack comes by default at AWS, and it is free.

In addition to default metrics published by AWS Services, you can also publish your own metrics and leverage CloudWatch's features.

Configuring advanced CloudWatch alarms

The most powerful feature of CloudWatch are alarms. Alarms are triggers that are executed in response to CloudWatch events. For example, you can set up an alarm that is triggered when **TotalErrorRate** metric for our CloudFront distribution exceeds some threshold.

To create an alarm easily, you can click the **Create alarm** button (ring icon) on the **Graphed metrics** tab. Please now find the CloudFront's **TotalErrorRate** metric, select it and change to the **Graphed metrics** tab, and click to the **Create alarm** button. You will see the following screen:

Here, you should fill **Name** field, and in the **Actions** section you should select the **ServerlessBookDown** topic. After that, you need to click the **+ Notification** button, and this time you should select **State is OK** for the **Whenever this alarm** value and the same SNS topic. The tricky part is to determine the threshold. For this example, we picked is >= **5** for **1 consecutive period(s)**. This means whenever the error rate exceeds 5% for 5 minutes, the alarm will be triggered. You can play with these values according to your needs.

Now create the alarm and revert the change we did to the API Gateway endpoint, so put again authorization. After 5 minutes, as our health checkers will start to get error responses, you will observe this on the graph, and also the alarm will be triggered, so you will get an SMS.

You should have realized what a powerful feature this is. As you know, you can trigger almost anything with SNS, and CloudWatch alarms are also triggering SNS topics. This means that the sky is the limit for any orchestration of cloud events. For example, you can write a Lambda function that sends Slack messages to your team, and this function can be invoked when endless number of events happen in your application. Moreover, you do not need high integration efforts to have such a great monitoring solution.

One small thing left about alarms: our health check did not send us any message when it became healthy again. It was because for that alarm, the `State is OK` event was not configured by default. Now you can find that alarm, add this notification rule, and you will see that you will get notifications for downtime and when your application comes back online.

Wrapping everything up in CloudFormation

We can easily create the same endpoint using a CloudFormation template. Let's just add this block to the CloudFormation template's `Resources` section:

```
"TestEndpointHealthCheck": {
  "Type": "AWS::Route53::HealthCheck",
  "Properties": {
    "HealthCheckConfig": {
      "Port": "443",
      "Type": "HTTPS",
      "ResourcePath": "/test",
      "FullyQualifiedDomainName": {
        "Ref": "DomainName"
      },
      "RequestInterval": "30",
      "FailureThreshold": "3",
      "MeasureLatency": "true",
```

```
      "EnableSNI": "true"
    },
    "HealthCheckTags": [
      {
        "Key": "Name",
        "Value": "TestEndpoint"
      }
    ]
  }
}
```

This configuration will only create the health check, but it will not create the alarm. To have the same configuration we've just had with the UI, we need to create first an SNS topic, its subscriptions, and finally, the alarm.

Here we have the topic definition with only email subscription:

```
"HealthChecksSnsTopic": {
  "Type": "AWS::SNS::Topic",
    "Properties": {
    "Subscription": [
      {
          "Endpoint": "info@example.com",
          "Protocol": "email"
      }
    ]
  }
}
```

You can add SMS notification to this configuration by just replacing email address with SMS and your phone number with email address:

```
"HealthChecksAlarm": {
  "Type": "AWS::CloudWatch::Alarm",
  "Properties": {
    "ActionsEnabled": true,
    "AlarmDescription": "Alert when Health Check is down",
    "ComparisonOperator": "LessThanThreshold",
    "Dimensions": [
      {
        "Name": "HealthCheckId",
        "Value": {
          "Ref": "TestEndpointHealthCheck"
        }
      }
    ],
    "EvaluationPeriods": "3",
    "MetricName": "HealthCheckStatus",
```

```
      "Namespace": "AWS/Route53",
      "Period": "60",
      "Statistic": "Minimum",
      "Threshold": "1",
      "AlarmActions": [
        {
          "Ref": "HealthChecksSnsTopic"
        }
      ],
      "OKActions": [
        {
          "Ref": "HealthChecksSnsTopic"
        }
      ]
    }
  }
}
```

That's it, our health check is ready to use.

Now let's add also another alarm for high error rates:

```
"HighErrorRateAlarm": {
  "Type": "AWS::CloudWatch::Alarm",
    "Properties": {
      "ActionsEnabled": true,
      "AlarmDescription": "Alert when error rate is > 5%",
      "ComparisonOperator": "GreaterThanThreshold",
      "Dimensions": [
        {
          "Name": "Region",
          "Value": "Global"
        },
        {
          "Name": "DistributionId",
          "Value": {
            "Ref": "CloudformationDistribution"
          }
        }
      ],
      "MetricName": "TotalErrorRate",
      "EvaluationPeriods": "1",
      "Namespace": "AWS/CloudFront",
      "Period": "300",
      "Statistic": "Average",
      "Threshold": "5",
      "AlarmActions": [
        {
          "Ref": "HealthChecksSnsTopic"
```

```
      }
    ],
    "OKActions": [
      {
        "Ref": "HealthChecksSnsTopic"
      }
    ]
  }
}
```

This configuration is pretty same as health check alarm, but we have changed some key configuration fields; for example in namespace we set `AWS/Cloudfront`, and we changed the **Period** and **EvaluationPeriods** fields to set our alarm to be triggered for the calculated average metric of 5 minutes period. Also we changed the **Dimensions** and **MetricName** fields. Actually, this configuration did not come from memory; we can check the existing alarm we created via AWS Console and it is easy to find these values.

Creating CloudWatch metrics from application logs

As we've seen before, Lambda functions save their log events to CloudWatch. This lets us to watch our application's status easily, and we do not have to maintain any logging infrastructure for that. This is already a cool feature.

If you've ever used a logging solution such as Kibana, you should be familiar with saving search patterns in it, so you can create graphs using the occurrence frequency of a pattern in your logs. This is possible to have some functionality very easily in CloudWatch logs. This feature is called **Create Metric Filter** and automatically tests custom patterns against log lines and pushes them as a metric to CloudWatch. With that, for example, you can see how many times your log contained an ERROR string, you can monitor it via CloudWatch graphics, or you can even create alarms and take action when your application error rate is very high.

To set up a metric filter, you can click to the **Logs** link on CloudWatch console. As our TestLambda is being invoked continuously because we set up Route53 Health Check, you can already see the log group belonging to the TestLambda function. Now you can click on it and explore the log events:

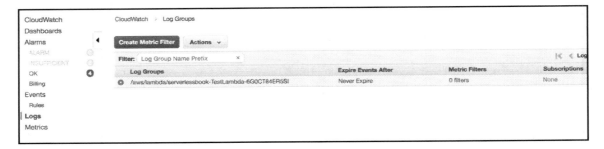

To create a metric filter, you can select the log and click on the **Create Metric Filter** button.

On the next screen, you are shown some selected events from the log file and asked to enter a filter pattern:

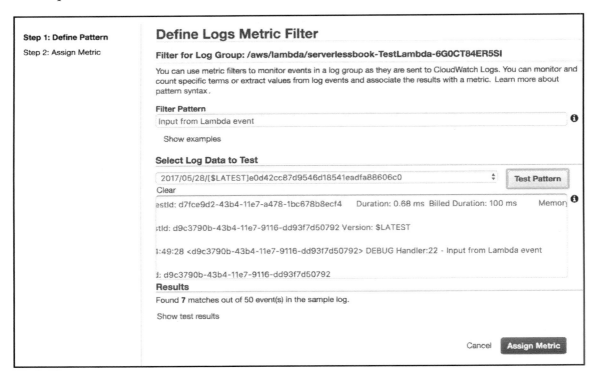

As you remember, in our code, we wrote a logging instruction that always pushes `Input from Lambda event` text into the log. We can use this string to see how many times our Lambda is invoked, so let's write this text in the **Filter Pattern** box and click on the **Assign Metric** button to skip to the next step.

 It does not make any sense to create such a filter just to see how many times our Lambda is invoked because by default we have such a metric that we can use. This feature is for application events, so when you write more log events in your application, you can create a metric using that event. It is up to you.

On the next screen we are asked to enter a **Filter Name**, **Metric Namespace**, and **Metric Name** value:

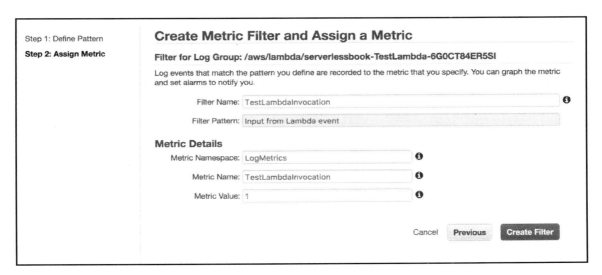

You can write whatever value you want, just be careful to decide about a namespace value so you can see all your application log metrics in one place. After you write the values, you can click on **Create Filter** button and create the metric.

After waiting a bit, you can click on **Metrics** and see that your logs are being analyzed and the results are being printed on the graph:

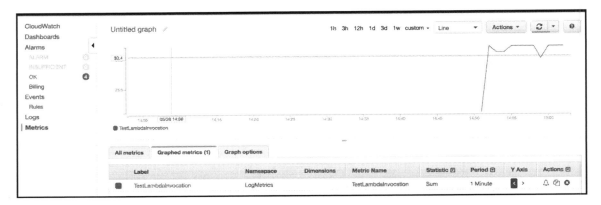

Now, just remember that you can create an alarm, then this alarm can send an event to a SNS topic, and from there you can invoke another Lambda function, send notification to different mediums (email, SMS, even push notification for mobile device) and so on. This is the power of AWS: there are tools and it is up to you how to glue them.

Running Lambda functions in VPC

VPC (Virtual Private Cloud) is an important part of AWS: it is a private network that you can create for your account and it gives you very granular control of your networking needs. You can create subnets, assign IP addresses to your EC2 instances from these subnets, and adjust security settings to allow or block access from specific subnets.

Actually, every AWS account has a default VPC when you open the account. When you create an EC2 instance, you select a subnet from your default subnets and your instance is given a private IP address. While you create an instance, you can also give a public IP to your instance, so that your instance can be accessed from the public internet. But in a secured environment, you should assign only a private IP to your instance and block access to your instance from the public internet. In this case, you have a couple of options to access these resources: create a VPN connection to your VPC, or create a bastion host with public internet access, so you can open a SSH tunnel to that host and then access other hosts in VPC.

When your instance does not have a public IP, it also does not have outgoing Internet access, so in this case you need to create a NAT Gateway in your VPC that translates outgoing internet connection to your VPC.

In corporate environments where AWS is in use, the most of resources are placed into VPC so security is ensured at the network level. One of the typical examples of VPC-protected resources is **RDS (Relational Database Service)** instances.

 Although you have an option to put them in public IP space, it is a very bad idea from a security perspective because anybody who has credentials and the public IP address of your RDS instance can access to your company's data. Therefore it is always a good practice to place RDS instances to VPC and not assign them a public IP.

In larger organisations, it is the best practice to place each different application in a separate AWS account. This provides more separation of different services and is good from people organisation perspective. Here's an example that the author of this book experienced: you are working in a company where ten different teams are providing different microservices and you are responsible to build a serverless application that aggregates information from those services. Every team is operating on different AWS accounts and for their microservices they refuse to open access to public IPs, but they ask you to give specific IP addresses, so they can only allow connections originating from those addresses. On the other hand, you never know which IP address Lambda is using when it connects to outer internet because of the distributed nature of Lambda.

This scenario is very common, and until VPC support came to Lambda in the beginning of 2016, it was a big headache. Fortunately, now we can run our Lambda in a specific VPC and let them get an IP address from a specified subnet in our VPC. To solve the previous scenario, we need to create a NAT Gateway in our VPC, so we ensure that any connection to outer internet goes through this gateway, so we can tell our colleagues from other teams to allow access to NAT Gateway's IP address, so our Lambda function can access their services.

Creating a VPC

In this section, we will create a VPC consisting of two private and two public subnets. Both subnets will be distributed among two availability zone in the region our application works. From the AWS perspective, it is a good idea to remind that all subnets are just a pool of IP addresses. What makes a subnet public is a routing rule that routes traffic to Internet Gateway. Internet Gateway is also a AWS component that bridges outer internet with our VPC.

We will then install two NAT Gateways on both public subnets. Both private subnets will have a routing rule that moves the outgoing internet traffic to NAT Gateway, so NAT Gateways can enable communication between those private subnets with outer Internet. On the other hand, resources in the private subnet will not be accessible from outer internet, so they will stay secure. We will create two Elastic IPs which are available from internet. These IP addresses will be assigned to NAT Gateways. Whenever a host in a private subnet accesses internet resource, the traffic will be seen as originating from those Elastic IP addresses. It means that we need to give those IP addresses to other teams if we want them to allow their service to access our application.

 NAT Gateways are billed per hour and data transfer. Whenever you create them you will be started to billed, so when you do not need them, remove them. We could also create only one NAT Gateway and share it between two private subnets. This is possible and might seem a cheaper solution. On the other hand, if the region where NAT Gateway goes down, that your application will lose Internet connectivity. That's why we play it safe and create two NAT Gateways.

Now let's start to create our VPC config. This part may seem a bit complicated if you do not have networking knowledge. If you do not understand any term you can refer to the AWS VPC documentation.

To start the VPC configuration, first we need to add a VPC itself:

```
"VPC": {
  "Type": "AWS::EC2::VPC",
    "Properties": {
      "CidrBlock": "10.0.0.0/16",
      "Tags": [
        {
          "Key": "Name",
          "Value": {
            "Fn::Sub": "${AWS::StackName}: VPC"
          }
        }
```

```
        ]
      }
  }
```

Our VPC will span 10.0.0.0/16 IP Block. As you know from CIDR notation, this IP range starts from 10.0.0.0 and ends at 10.0.255.255, meaning that our subnets under this VPC should be inside this range.

Adding private subnets

Now we need to add two private subnets under this VPC:

```
"PrivateSubnet1": {
  "Type": "AWS::EC2::Subnet",
    "Properties": {
    "VpcId": {
      "Ref": "VPC"
    },
    "CidrBlock": "10.0.1.0/24",
    "AvailabilityZone": {
      "Fn::Select": [ "0",
        {
          "Fn::GetAZs": {
            "Ref": "AWS::Region"
          }
        }
      ]
    },
    "Tags": [
      {
        "Key": "Name",
        "Value": {
          "Fn::Sub": "${AWS::StackName}: Private Subnet 1"
        }
      }
    ]
  }
},
"PrivateSubnet2": {
  "Type": "AWS::EC2::Subnet",
    "Properties": {
    "VpcId": {
      "Ref": "VPC"
    },
    "CidrBlock": "10.0.3.0/24",
    "AvailabilityZone": {
```

```json
      "Fn::Select": [
        "1",
        {
          "Fn::GetAZs": {
            "Ref": "AWS::Region"
          }
        }
      ]
    },
    "Tags": [
      {
        "Key": "Name",
        "Value": {
          "Fn::Sub": "${AWS::StackName}: Private Subnet 2"
        }
      }
    ]
  }
}
```

Here we tell the VPC to create subnets. For the first subnet, we select a CIDR block that starts from 10.0.1.0 and ends at 10.0.1.255. For the second one we select a block from 10.0.3.0 to 10.0.3.255. Each subnet has 256 available IP addresses.

Note the usage of the Fn::GetAZs method. For both subnets, we get the first and second availability zones of the region, so we distribute our IP pool among two different availability zones.

 Although availability zones are physical zones, they are independently mapped identifiers for each account. For example, your Availability Zone us-east-1a might not be the same location as us-east-1a for another account. So for every account, the first and second availability zones will be different. Here, we only create two subnets because every region has a minimum two availability zones. If you are sure that you are installing your stack in a region where more than two availability zones exist, you can increase the number of subnets.

With this configuration, we ensure that our Lambda functions, when we configure them to operate in VPC, will get one of those IP addresses automatically. On the other hand, we have to remember that we have a important limit: as our available IP address count is 512 (256 for each availability zone). Our maximum Lambda execution count is also limited to 512. To increase this number, you have to adjust the subnets so they have sufficient IP addresses for parallel executions.

After the private subnets, we also create two public subnets. While Lambda functions are in private subnets, NAT Gateways will be placed in public subnets. Public subnets are also routed to the internet, so any resource that you place in a public subnet, can also have a internet IP address and thus access to outer Internet. Moreover, they are also able to connect to any subnet in the same VPC. It means, when we place NAT Gateway into a public gateway, they can access internet and Lambda functions. That's why NAT Gateways are able to act as a NAT device and provide internet connectivity to Lambda functions while Lambda functions are not accessible from outside internet.

Let's now create public subnets. Actually their configuration is same as private subnet, but they are routed to Internet Gateway, which makes them public subnet. First, let's create them. After that we will see how to connect them to internet:

```
"PublicSubnet1": {
  "Type": "AWS::EC2::Subnet",
    "Properties": {
      "VpcId": {
        "Ref": "VPC"
      },
      "CidrBlock": "10.0.0.0/24",
      "AvailabilityZone": {
        "Fn::Select": [
          "0",
          {
            "Fn::GetAZs": {
              "Ref": "AWS::Region"
            }
          }
        ]
      },
      "Tags": [
        {
          "Key": "Name",
          "Value": {
            "Fn::Sub": "${AWS::StackName}: Public Subnet 1"
          }
        }
      ]
    }
},
"PublicSubnet2": {
  "Type": "AWS::EC2::Subnet",
    "Properties": {
      "VpcId": {
        "Ref": "VPC"
      },
      "CidrBlock": "10.0.2.0/24",
```

```
        "AvailabilityZone": {
          "Fn::Select": [
            "1",
            {
              "Fn::GetAZs": {
                "Ref": "AWS::Region"
              }
            }
          ]
        },
        "Tags": [
          {
            "Key": "Name",
            "Value": {
              "Fn::Sub": "${AWS::StackName}: Public Subnet 2 "
            }
          }
        ]
      }
    }
  }
```

Before we deal with public subnets, let's create two route tables for private subnets and associate them with private subnets:

```
"PrivateRouteTable1": {
  "Type": "AWS::EC2::RouteTable",
  "Properties": {
    "VpcId": {
      "Ref": "VPC"
    },
    "Tags": [
      {
        "Key": "Name",
        "Value": {
          "Fn::Sub": "${AWS::StackName}: Route Table for Private Subnet 1 "
        }
      }
    ]
  }
},
"PrivateRouteTable2": {
  "Type": "AWS::EC2::RouteTable",
  "Properties": {
    "VpcId": {
      "Ref": "VPC"
    },
    "Tags": [
      {
```

```
        "Key": "Name",
          "Value": {
            "Fn::Sub": "${AWS::StackName}: Route Table for Private Subnet 2"
          }
        }
      ]
    }
  },
  "PrivateSubnetRouteTableAssociation1": {
    "Type": "AWS::EC2::SubnetRouteTableAssociation",
    "Properties": {
      "SubnetId": {
        "Ref": "PrivateSubnet1"
      },
      "RouteTableId": {
        "Ref": "PrivateRouteTable1"
      }
    }
  },
  "PrivateSubnetRouteTableAssociation2": {
    "Type": "AWS::EC2::SubnetRouteTableAssociation",
    "Properties": {
      "SubnetId": {
        "Ref": "PrivateSubnet2"
      },
      "RouteTableId": {
        "Ref": "PrivateRouteTable2"
      }
    }
  }
}
```

The syntax here is not very complicated. Route tables are rule tables for routing a subnet. When we create our NAT Gateways, we will add rules to these tables, so any outgoing traffic originating from these subnets are routed to NAT Gateways.

In the same way, let's create a single route table for both public subnets and associate subnets with it in the same way:

```
"PublicRouteTable": {
  "Type": "AWS::EC2::RouteTable",
    "Properties": {
      "VpcId": {
        "Ref": "VPC"
      },
      "Tags": [
        {
          "Key": "Name",
          "Value": {
```

```
                "Fn::Sub": "${AWS::StackName}: Route Table for Public Subnet"
              }
            }
          ]
        }
    },
    "PublicSubnetRouteTableAssociation1": {
      "Type": "AWS::EC2::SubnetRouteTableAssociation",
      "Properties": {
        "SubnetId": {
          "Ref": "PublicSubnet1"
        },
        "RouteTableId": {
          "Ref": "PublicRouteTable"
        }
      }
    },
    "PublicSubnetRouteTableAssociation2": {
      "Type": "AWS::EC2::SubnetRouteTableAssociation",
      "Properties": {
        "SubnetId": {
          "Ref": "PublicSubnet2"
        },
        "RouteTableId": {
          "Ref": "PublicRouteTable"
        }
      }
    },
```

We did not need two route tables here because in this table we will only have one rule, which routes the outgoing traffic to Internet Gateway.

Port traffic in VPC is controlled via **Access Control Lists (ACLs)**. With ACL, you can limit the network traffic at a lower level, without having to deal with security groups. In our case, we will open all the traffic for all ports.

Now we create a **ACL** and associate it with public subnets:

```
    "PublicNetworkAcl": {
      "Type": "AWS::EC2::NetworkAcl",
      "Properties": {
        "VpcId": {
          "Ref": "VPC"
        },
        "Tags": [
          {
            "Key": "Name",
            "Value": {
```

```
              "Fn::Sub": "${AWS::StackName}: Public Network ACL"
            }
          }
        ]
      }
    },

    "PublicSubnetNetworkAclAssociation1": {
      "Type": "AWS::EC2::SubnetNetworkAclAssociation",
      "Properties": {
        "SubnetId": {
          "Ref": "PublicSubnet1"
        },
        "NetworkAclId": {
          "Ref": "PublicNetworkAcl"
        }
      }
    },
    "PublicSubnetNetworkAclAssociation2": {
      "Type": "AWS::EC2::SubnetNetworkAclAssociation",
      "Properties": {
        "SubnetId": {
          "Ref": "PublicSubnet2"
        },
        "NetworkAclId": {
          "Ref": "PublicNetworkAcl"
        }
      }
    }
  }
```

Handling inbound and outbound traffic

Once we have the ACL created and associated with public subnets, we can allow all inbound and outbound traffic for that:

```
"OutboundPublicNetworkAclEntry": {
  "Type": "AWS::EC2::NetworkAclEntry",
  "Properties": {
    "NetworkAclId": {
      "Ref": "PublicNetworkAcl"
    },
    "RuleNumber": "100",
    "Protocol": "6",
    "RuleAction": "allow",
    "Egress": "true",
    "CidrBlock": "0.0.0.0/0",
```

```
      "PortRange": {
        "From": "0",
        "To": "65535"
      }
    }
  },
  "InboundPublicNetworkAclEntry": {
    "Type": "AWS::EC2::NetworkAclEntry",
    "Properties": {
      "NetworkAclId": {
        "Ref": "PublicNetworkAcl"
      },
      "RuleNumber": "100",
      "Protocol": "6",
      "RuleAction": "allow",
      "Egress": "false",
      "CidrBlock": "0.0.0.0/0",
      "PortRange": {
        "From": "0",
        "To": "65535"
      }
    }
  },
```

You can get more information about this resource's syntax at
`http://docs.aws.amazon.com/AWSCloudFormation/latest/UserGuide/aws-resource-ec2-network-acl-entry.html`. Especially for the `Protocol` property you might need to check the documentation. Just to be clear, 6 means TCP traffic here, as defined at
`http://www.iana.org/assignments/protocol-numbers/protocol-numbers.xhtml`.
Alternatively, can use -1 for all protocols.

 In VPC, ACLs are stateless unlike security groups. Security groups are stateful. If you add an inbound rule for port 80 for a security group, the traffic is automatically allowed out, meaning an outbound rule for that particular port need not be explicitly added. But with ACLs you need to provide explicit inbound and outbound rules. That's why we also defined an inbound rule.

Now, we have to create an Internet Gateway and route all outgoing traffic from the public subnet to that Internet Gateway:

```
"InternetGateway": {
  "Type": "AWS::EC2::InternetGateway",
  "Properties": {
    "Tags": [
      {
        "Key": "Name",
        "Value": {
          "Fn::Sub": "${AWS::StackName}: Internet Gateway"
        }
      }
    ]
  }
},
"GatewayToInternet": {
  "Type": "AWS::EC2::VPCGatewayAttachment",
  "Properties": {
    "VpcId": {
      "Ref": "VPC"
    },
    "InternetGatewayId": {
      "Ref": "InternetGateway"
    }
  }
},
"PublicRoute": {
  "Type": "AWS::EC2::Route",
  "DependsOn": "GatewayToInternet",
  "Properties": {
    "RouteTableId": {
      "Ref": "PublicRouteTable"
    },
    "DestinationCidrBlock": "0.0.0.0/0",
    "GatewayId": {
      "Ref": "InternetGateway"
    }
  }
}
```

Right now, we have ensured that any device with an IP at public subnet will have internet access because all traffic is routed to Internet Gateway. Now we create Elastic IP addresses (Internet-accessible IPs) and create NAT Gateways. We will attach the Elastic IP with the NAT Gateway, and then we will create a routing rule that routes all private subnet to NAT Gateways. Note that the first private subnet will be routed to the first NAT Gateway and the second one to the second NAT Gateway:

```
"EIP1": {
  "Type": "AWS::EC2::EIP",
  "Properties": {
    "Domain": "vpc"
  }
},
"NAT1": {
  "DependsOn": "GatewayToInternet",
  "Type": "AWS::EC2::NatGateway",
  "Properties": {
    "AllocationId": {
      "Fn::GetAtt": [
        "EIP1",
        "AllocationId"
      ]
    },
    "SubnetId": {
      "Ref": "PublicSubnet1"
    }
  }
},
"Nat1Route": {
  "Type": "AWS::EC2::Route",
  "Properties": {
    "RouteTableId": {
      "Ref": "PrivateRouteTable1"
    },
    "DestinationCidrBlock": "0.0.0.0/0",
    "NatGatewayId": {
      "Ref": "NAT1"
    }
  }
}
```

And now, let's create the second NAT Gateway in pretty much the same way:

```
"Nat2Route": {
  "Type": "AWS::EC2::Route",
  "Properties": {
    "RouteTableId": {
```

```
        "Ref": "PrivateRouteTable2"
      },
      "DestinationCidrBlock": "0.0.0.0/0",
      "NatGatewayId": {
        "Ref": "NAT2"
      }
    }
  },
  "EIP2": {
    "Type": "AWS::EC2::EIP",
    "Properties": {
      "Domain": "vpc"
    }
  },
  "NAT2": {
    "DependsOn": "GatewayToInternet",
    "Type": "AWS::EC2::NatGateway",
    "Properties": {
      "AllocationId": {
        "Fn::GetAtt": [
          "EIP2",
          "AllocationId"
        ]
      },
      "SubnetId": {
        "Ref": "PublicSubnet2"
      }
    }
  },
  "EIP2": {
    "Type": "AWS::EC2::EIP",
    "Properties": {
      "Domain": "vpc"
    }
  },
  "Nat1Route": {
    "Type": "AWS::EC2::Route",
    "Properties": {
      "RouteTableId": {
        "Ref": "PrivateRouteTable1"
      },
      "DestinationCidrBlock": "0.0.0.0/0",
      "NatGatewayId": {
        "Ref": "NAT1"
      }
    }
  }
}
```

When you deploy the stack, it will create the VPC and everything else for you.

Creating a Security Group

Before we continue with Lambda functions' VPC configurations we also need to create a Security Group. Like network ACLs, Security Groups are logical security groups that you assign to your resources and you can allow or deny incoming or outgoing traffic. Contrary to ACL's, you assign security groups to resources, not to subnets. For our Lamba functions we do not specify any incoming traffic rule, because they cannot accept incoming traffic. However, we need to specify an outgoing traffic rule which will allow all traffic out. Let's add the following resource to your template:

```
"LambdaSecurityGroup": {
  "Type": "AWS::EC2::SecurityGroup",
  "Properties": {
    "GroupDescription": "Security Group for Lambda Functions",
    "VpcId": {
      "Ref": "VPC"
    },
    "SecurityGroupIngress": [
    ],
    "SecurityGroupEgress": [
      {
          "IpProtocol": "-1",
        "FromPort": "0",
        "ToPort": "65535",
        "CidrIp": "0.0.0.0/0"
      }
    ]
  }
}
```

After adding the security group config for each Lambda function you have, add this configuration to the Properties field:

```
"VpcConfig": {
  "SecurityGroupIds": [
    {
      "Ref": "LambdaSecurityGroup"
    }
  ],
  "SubnetIds": [
    {
      "Ref": "PrivateSubnet1"
    },
```

```
{
    "Ref": "PrivateSubnet2"
}
]
```

With this configuration, you tell AWS to run your Lambda function inside one of the subnets you specify and apply the indicated security group to its networking configuration.

After we deploy the stack, our application should still be running as expected, with one difference: the outgoing Internet requests now go through NAT Gateway. Maybe you did not realize, but actually our application heavily uses outgoing Internet connections because DynamoDB and CloudSearch APIs are in public internet, so without NAT Gateway and with VPC Config, our application would break.

Can you now try to register a user, then remove NAT Gateway, or basically Nat1Route and Nat2Route resources and make sure that when you remove routes your application doesn't work because it can't connect to AWS APIs?

Now you can navigate to the VPC page of AWS Console, click **NAT Gateways**, and see the Elastic IP addresses of your NAT Gateways:

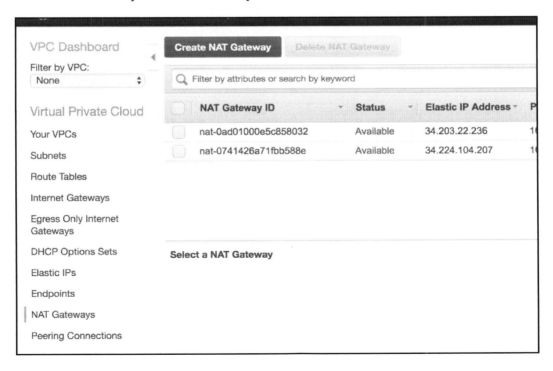

These are the IP addresses that you need to tell your colleagues for allowing access. Now, your Lambda functions will be able to access that firewall-protected resource, and nobody else will.

Summary

In this chapter, we mentioned about how to monitor and secure your serverless application. Especially, VPC is a very complicated topic, but it is extremely important once you try to build serverless software in the enterprise domain.

This was our last chapter and we have finished a long journey, congratulations! We hope you enjoyed it and are now able to write your own serverless software without worrying about your infrastructure needs any more.

We are also aware that we could not cover everything we wanted because AWS is a huge area and we wanted to cover as much as possible. We hope we have encouraged you to explore more and solve your problems in more creative ways.

Lambda Framework

So far we built our application specifically for Lambda functions. However many times we already have some application built and running on an on-premise infrastructure and we want to give a try to serverless architecture, or we want to build our software infrastructure agnostic, so when we need this, we want to switch back to our own infrastructure with minimum code change.

Getting to know Lambda Framework

Lambda Framework was created for this use case. Lambda Framework accomplishes this target by implementing the most common JAX-RS annotations and providing a Maven plugin to deploy easily to the AWS cloud. Briefly, JAX-RS is a standard annotation set of J2EE which can be used to map regular Java methods to HTTP paths and methods. For instance, you can look at the following method:

```
@GET
@Path("/helloworld/{id}")
public Response indexEndpoint(@PathParam int id) {
    return Response.status(200).entity("Hello world: " + id).build();
}
```

This is a very lean method marked with the `@GET` and `@Path` annotations, which mean that this method is called when a GET request comes to URLs in the `/helloworld/{id}` format, with the `id` parameter as an argument. Finally, it returns a `Response` object within this method with a 200 response code and text content. As you can see, these annotations offer a seamless way to define a REST API and map different resources to Java methods.

JAX-RS annotations on their own do not mean so much and they do not have any effect out-of-the-box. To make these annotations work, a JAX-RS implementation framework should be added to the project. This framework would scan all the JAX-RS annotations in the project and create a server and routing table to respond to HTTP requests correctly. While Jersey is one such reference implementation, and the most popular one, there are also other implementations of JAX-RS, such as RESTEasy and Apache CXF. You are free to choose any of them and your controller methods will always stay the same, thanks to standard annotations.

Lambda Framework is a JAX-RS implementation but different from the others: instead of running a web server, it scans the JAX-RS annotations at build time and populates Lambda functions and the API Gateway definitions using them.

This means that if you have already marked your controller methods with JAX-RS annotations and used a framework such as Jersey or RestEasy, you can easily switch to a serverless architecture with very few modifications in your code. You would have to change only your build mechanism and replace your preferred JAX-RS implementation with Lambda Framework.

To start working with Lambda Framework you can clone the boilerplate project provided by Lambda Framework itself. You can clone it using the following command:

```
$ git clone https://github.com/lambadaframework/
    lambadaframework-boilerplate
```

Let us check the `ExampleController` class inside this project:

```
@Path("/")
public class ExampleController {

  static final Logger logger = Logger.getLogger(ExampleController.class);
  static class Entity {
    public int id = 1;
    public String name;

    public Entity(String name) {
       this.name = name;
    }
  }

  @GET
  public Response indexEndpoint(
  ) {
    logger.debug("Request got");
    return Response.status(200)
    .entity(new Entity("John doe"))
```

```java
      .build();
  }

  @GET
  @Path("/{name}")
  public Response exampleEndpoint(
    @PathParam("name") String name
  ) {
    logger.debug("Request got");
    return Response.status(201)
    .entity(new Entity(name))
    .build();
  }

  @GET
  @Path("/resource/{name}")
  public Response exampleSecondEndpoint(
    @PathParam("name") String name
  ) {
    logger.debug("Request got");
    return Response.status(201)
    .entity(new Entity(name))
    .build();
  }

  public static class NewEntityRequest {
    public String name;
  }

  /**
   * This controller uses automatically serialization of Request body to
any POJO
   * @param requestEntity Request Entity
   * @return Response
   */
  @POST
  @Consumes(MediaType.APPLICATION_JSON)
  @Path("/resource")
  public Response exampleSecondEndpointPost(
     NewEntityRequest requestEntity
  ) {
    logger.debug("Request got");
    return Response.status(201)
    .entity(new Entity(requestEntity.name))
    .build();
  }
}
```

Here we are provided with some controller methods annotated with JAX-RS annotations. If we add a JAX-RS library such as Jersey to our project, this class would create a couple of REST endpoints for us. For example, the `/production/cagatay` path would return the following as JSON:

```
{
   id: 1,
   name: "cagatay"
}
```

This is how Lambda Framework does it. If you look at Maven's `pom.xml` file (yes, unfortunately Lambda uses Maven), there is one dependency injected into the project: `org.lambadaframework.runtime`. This package has a JAX-RS annotation processor and also creates a Lambda handler inside the final JAR package.

To deploy the project with Lambda, you need to edit only one variable in the `pom.xml` file, which is `deployment.package`. You need to write a name there which is unique to your project, because S3 buckets should be unique globally, as you know from past chapters.

When you are ready, you should fire the `mvn deploy` command. With this command your project is compiled and a fat JAR file with your code and Lambda's runtime routines is created and uploaded to a S3 bucket. After that, Lambda Framework's Maven plugin comes into the scene and creates the Lambda function for you. After that, it scans your project and determines the JAX-RS resources. API Gateway resources and methods are created using the specifications you define on the JAX-RS annotations.

After deployment finishes, your API's public URL is printed on the screen.

On Lambda Framework's Github page (`https://github.com/lambadaframework/lambadaframework`), you can also see a couple of configuration values.

Summary

Lambda Framework is suitable for migrating your existing REST API easily and also fast prototyping. You can benefit from it if it fits in your use case. On the other hand, as we have seen throughout this book, there are endless numbers of patterns and configuration values to be used with Lambda and maybe it is good idea to keep your controller layer simple and separated from your business logic and build custom Lambda handlers and Lambda functions.

Index